THRESHOLD
EDITIONS

# JUSTICE FOR ALL

## HOW THE LEFT IS WRONG ABOUT LAW ENFORCEMENT

# GREG KELLY

THRESHOLD
EDITIONS

New York    London    Toronto    Sydney    New Delhi

## THRESHOLD
## EDITIONS

An Imprint of Simon & Schuster, Inc.
1230 Avenue of the Americas
New York, NY 10020

First Threshold Editions hardcover edition January 2023

THRESHOLD EDITIONS and colophon are trademarks of Simon & Schuster, Inc.

For information about special discounts for bulk purchases,
please contact Simon & Schuster Special Sales at 1-866-506-1949
or business@simonandschuster.com.

The Simon & Schuster Speakers Bureau can bring authors
to your live event. For more information or to book an event,
contact the Simon & Schuster Speakers Bureau at 1-866-248-3049
or visit our website at www.simonspeakers.com.

Interior design by Erika R. Genova

Manufactured in the United States of America

1   3   5   7   9   10  8   6   4   2

Library of Congress Cataloging-in-Publication Data is available.

ISBN 978-1-6680-0202-5
ISBN 978-1-6680-0204-9 (ebook)

To my father,
Raymond W. Kelly,
the greatest police commissioner
to ever live and serve

# CONTENTS

# INTRODUCTION

THIS IS A BOOK ABOUT justice in America and the consequences to our beautiful nation if justice fails. Trust in law enforcement and the institutions of public safety has been hollowed out. The center pole of the American way of life is freedom, but liberty must be paired with respect for the rule of law or else we will descend into chaos. That's where America stands right now—at the edge of chaos.

Everyone feels it—I know I do. Don't you? Divisions have emerged that could tear America apart. We fail to agree on fundamental matters—such as: Are police bad? Is stealing harmless? Should white and black people be treated equally?—and it doesn't seem that we are close to repairing the rift.

The core of the problem, as I see it, is that there is a hideously dishonest conversation about race going on in America today in order to avoid some uncomfortable truths. I'm sick of listening to elected officials, media personalities, and radical advocates lie through their teeth about the reality of crime, criminal justice, and law enforcement in this country. The victims of this campaign of deep untruth include all of us, but it affects the men and women of law enforcement most grievously. They have been scapegoated, lied about, and savagely denigrated. Violence against cops is rising rapidly: the FBI says that murders of cops were up 59 percent during 2021, much higher than the figures for the nation at large.[1]

Almost every year or two, typically corresponding to the election cycle, some incident involving a police officer and a civilian—usually black—is amplified and magnified by the press, the national Democrat Party, and street-level "activists" to promote the idea that America is a racist dictatorship that feeds like a starving mosquito on the blood of African Americans. Civil unrest breaks out—sometimes locally, sometimes nationally—to agitate the base and convince a segment of the electorate that one half of the country is ignorant, backward, cruel, and "RACIST."

I lay the blame for this deeply false dynamic on Barack Obama. The senator from Illinois who consciously echoed Abraham Lincoln in his speeches, and who represented the promise of a "postracial America"—where people could get along normally and stop obsessing over skin color—turned out to be as wicked and divisive a race hustler as any street corner lunatic or Jim Crow–era segregationist sheriff. He got elected president in 2008 on the premise of uniting America, and then set about lighting fires of resentment and discord everywhere he could, using ancient fears as leverage to grab as much power as he could.

I wrote this book to lay out the case against Barack Obama, his politics of division, and the Democrat Party, which he continues to lead behind the scenes, and in support of the men and women of law enforcement. They deserve better, and so does America. At its core, American institutions exist to preserve public safety, the rule of law, and peaceable enjoyment of the fruits of one's labors. Yet these institutions are teetering on collapse. People of good conscience must agree now to fight to shore up the timbers of the American system; otherwise it is all going to fall apart and get washed into the tides of history.

## EARLY DAYS

I was five years old when I first saw my father take his gun out and threaten to shoot someone.

We had gone as a family, including my brother, who was eight, and my mother, who was in her late twenties, studying to be a nurse, to Times Square Stores in January 1974. The store was in Hempstead, the town next to ours, Baldwin, on Long Island, New York.

My father, Raymond Kelly, was a sergeant in the New York City Police Department, and he would ultimately serve as the department's commissioner, the leader of the force, a position he held for fourteen years: a record in the history of New York City.

But on that winter night, Ray Kelly was just a foot soldier in the army he would later command. He worked "undercover," which added mystery to the only vague idea I had about what he did. The shorthand was that he would go to "work" to "catch bad guys." But he often wore a tie and coat to work. I didn't really know how he spent his time, or what "work" looked like.

I knew something about the police from television, but my father didn't wear a uniform when he went to work. He looked very much like the men on TV, but not on the cop shows. This was Bob Newhart making his way home from the office, or Tony Randall as Felix Unger neatly attired, running errands in the opening credits of *The Odd Couple*.

But "catching bad guys" wasn't so amiable. As I was about to learn.

It was supposed to be a quick trip to the store. My mother went inside to return my brother's birthday gift, a toy aircraft carrier. It had a rudimentary remote control by which a child could guide model F-4 Phantom jets onto the deck. But despite looking awesome in the commercial, the toy was a disappointment at home. In fact, it didn't work at all.

We were parked directly outside the store. My brother and I were wrestling in the back seat, making some kind of ruckus, but my father had gone to *work*: he noticed a man lingering by the door, outside. Standing outdoors was unusual enough on such a cold night. If he was waiting for a ride, it could have been done from inside. Also, he was watching everyone coming in or out closely.

I was oblivious, until an explosion of speed. Our car zoomed from 0 to 60, it seemed, in a half second. I went airborne, before slamming into the floor. Looking up, I saw my brother in his red puffy jacket, seat belt on, petrified.

This car, which had never done anything more than bring us to school or to the shopping center, was now careening with a roar over traffic islands.

"What happened?!?!"

"Someone did something *bad*," my father said.

There it was. His work. Catching a bad guy. This is what he did. But this time, we were there.

The bad guy, the one my father had been watching by the department store entrance, had stolen a woman's purse and was running away.

And we saw him! He was concealing his face, keeping it away from us as he ran. A long coat, with a belt coming off it. Was he crying? Running and crying. Who is this? Why is he doing that?

He was tall, maybe six foot six, and had a tremendous gait. We were paralleling him, but he was a lane over. Opposite traffic. Chaos. He turned into some sort of clearing—a parking lot, maybe. And so did we.

"Stay here," my dad ordered us.

He didn't yell. I don't think I ever heard him yell growing up.

My father had his gun out. A revolver. Pointing it in his left hand. His arm at pants-pocket level.

There was some yelling then from whoever this was. Angry words. The man came closer to my father, irate, flailing his arms. He was shouting.

My father replied with something like a growl. It may have been profanity, which at that age, in that time, I didn't comprehend.

The robber suddenly looked scared, the way my brother or I might have looked if we realized we were running late for dinner, and had already been warned about being on time.

He dropped the purse and ran, back to where it was dark— a fence, shrubs, cars, mystery.

My father came back to the car with the pocketbook.

"What happened? What did he say?" we clamored.

"He said, 'Go ahead and shoot me, I have nothing to live for.'"

My brother and I were stunned. We'd never heard anything like that before.

I was holding the pocketbook, which seemed dull and ordinary, kind of lumpy. More like a knapsack than something my mother would carry.

On television, thieves stole jewels or robbed banks. They sought life-changing riches.

This handbag, on the other hand, seemed utterly mundane. What could be inside it: a pack of cigarettes, some gum, tissues? Maybe a hairbrush or some cheap makeup, a few dollars and some loose change.

A man had just risked his life to take this. For what? Nothing this woman was carrying could possibly be worth getting in trouble for . . . could it?

I was disappointed the bad guy had gotten away, and puzzled by what he had said.

*Go ahead and shoot me, I have nothing to live for.* In a way, that made sense, given the low stakes he was willing to play for, lurking outside a little department store and snatching a housewife's purse. It even sounded like something you might hear in an old gangster movie—Edward G. Robinson or Jimmy Cagney snarling *Come and get me, coppers* in a final act of rough bravado.

But even my five-year-old mind understood that there was no heroism in this thug's embittered plea. It was just desperate and grim.

"Why didn't you run after him?" my brother asked.

"Because you guys were here."

Back at the store, there seemed to be dozens of police cars.

When my mother came outside and found us, she saw us standing next to a police officer, and according to her, we were both crying. My father was in the back of a police car. It didn't look good; I can only imagine what kind of scenario went through her mind.

We filled her in soon enough. It was wild. It was interesting. It was dangerous. It was fun. I was thrilled by it all.

And I was deeply impressed by how my father handled it, especially how he was done talking about it by the time we got home, which was maybe a ten-minute drive from the store.

He was nonchalant because chasing after criminals was literally his life, his day job, not a special, once-in-a-lifetime-crazy spectacle. As an NYPD sergeant he had headed an anti-crime unit. He would work undercover, in "plain clothes," with a team of smart, aggressive cops, looking for crime, especially robberies, and interrupting it.

Later that year, Ray Kelly would be promoted to lieutenant after passing a competitive civil service test, another rung up the management ladder. By this time, he had also completed law school, passed the bar, earned a master's from New York University, fought in Vietnam as a Marine Corps officer, purchased a house, gotten married, and had two children.

My youth growing up in Nassau County on Long Island in the 1970s and '80s was normal. The fact that my father was a New York

City police officer was unusual among my friends, but it wasn't exceptional. It was his job—other kids' dads were contractors or bookkeepers, schoolteachers or grocers, and mine was a police officer.

Where I grew up was a typical kind of suburb, mostly white. American society at that time, and even now, had a certain degree of segregation built into its housing patterns. Some of it is the result of historical factors, but a lot of it is based on personal preference.

Sometimes liberals of my acquaintance will point to a building or neighborhood and remark how few black people live there, as though that means they have been kept out. "What makes you so sure black people want to live there?" I have asked occasionally. Not to sound like a wiseass, but why do white liberals assume that black people necessarily want to live where *they* live?

That's kind of typical of the liberal perspective, in my experience. They are so certain of their own perfection, they assume everyone is jealous of them. Having been around the world, first as a Marine and then as a broadcast reporter, I've seen enough places and been in enough cultures to understand that most people are happy enough being who they are—they aren't all itching to become a white liberal who listens to NPR and feeds her cat a vegan diet.

In any case, my father's work in the NYPD, as a precinct commander and then higher up in the organization, meant that he and my mother would entertain frequently. I remember many barbecues and parties with his work colleagues, and they were all a varied bunch. Black, white, Hispanic, some Asians . . . many religions. There was no tension or division. Everyone mixed as equals.

There are white people in this country who never really mix with people of other races—sometimes because of geography, sometimes just by circumstance or choice—but that wasn't my family. I had black friends; my parents had black friends. I remember visiting my father downtown, and a motorcycle officer, a black guy, gave me a ride on his bike. I loved it, and thought that he was the coolest guy in the world.

It's funny that saying "I have black friends" has become, to sneering liberals, the evidence that someone is "racist." But the fact is that the type of people who serve in the military, play sports, drive trucks, or otherwise work with their hands tend to interact with people of different races more frequently and consistently than the white liberals who make this obnoxious inference.

During this era, there were so many police funerals. In those days, a lot more cops were shot and killed than they are today. In 1972, there was a famous assassination of two NYPD officers that has faded from memory. Gregory Foster and Rocco Laurie were young guys, black and white, in their early twenties, patrolling the East Village. Today, Avenue B and 11th Street is tony and expensive, with million-dollar apartments and wine bars. But fifty years ago Alphabet City was basically one of the worst neighborhoods in New York.

Foster and Laurie were approached from behind by suspected members of the Black Liberation Army, who shot them dead and stole their guns. The BLA was a radical terrorist group that sought to "take up arms for the liberation and self-determination of black people in the United States." They were implicated in seventy acts of violence in the early seventies and the murder of thirteen police officers. But who remembers them today?

Gregory Foster was only twenty-two; his murder left behind a widow and two children. His grandson, also named Gregory Foster, today works the Ninth Precinct and wears his grandfather's badge number. Rocco Laurie was twenty-three. His wife, Adelaide, describes her husband's murder as a "wound that will never heal."

The officers' murders and funeral were a big deal. There's a famous picture of their widows sitting side by side, grieving, clutching wooden shields commemorating their slain husbands. The picture of two young widows, one black, one white, united in their grief, was splashed all over the papers and expressed a key message: the forces of chaos, disorder, and division may disguise themselves as movements of liberation, but their victims come from all walks of life. The idea of a "thin blue line" that protects society from the depredations of the criminal element has a truth to it, and that also means that law enforcement officers may have different-color skin, but they all bleed blue.

My father moved easily with people of all races. Part of that came from his military experience. He served in Vietnam as an officer in the Marines. When you are in the military, you work with a cross section of America. You have people of different races below you, next to you, and above you. What matters in terms of authority and respect are professionalism and unity of purpose, irrespective of race.

## TRULY EQUAL

My parents raised me to treat everyone I meet as my equal. Not that everyone is equally good at sports or math, or equally tall or pretty. But equal in the eyes of God. I think this is the key lesson of America, as stated in the Declaration of Independence. "We hold these truths to be self-evident, that all men are created equal, that they are endowed by their Creator with certain unalienable Rights, that among these are Life, Liberty and the Pursuit of Happiness."

This is the essential American creed and packs a lifetime's philosophy into a few dozen words. We are "created equal," meaning that we are each a God-made individual specimen of our type. That is to say, we are *special*, as members of a *species*. We are simultaneously unique and the same. We are entitled to certain rights, because everyone else is, too.

Martin Luther King Jr. offered a perfect restatement of Thomas Jefferson's immortal language when he said, 187 years later, that he envisioned a world where people are judged "by the content of their character" rather than "by the color of their skin." To me, this is also "self-evident." Everyone knows this to be true, and it is the basic teaching of all religions. What we look like from the outside doesn't matter: all that matters is our *character*, which is expressed through our words and actions.

Like everyone else in my generation and later, I absorbed this sentiment early on. I was the generation that grew up on *Sesame Street* and *Mister Rogers' Neighborhood*. For my whole life, the principles of racial equality, fairness, and a level playing field were drummed into me from every corner of society. I believed it then, and I believe it now. It makes sense.

I grew up, like most Americans, with a firm sense that everybody deserves to be treated on his own merits and that it's bad to prejudge anyone based on superficial matters like skin color. "I don't see color" used to be considered a noble sentiment; now it's thought to be a cynical mask for preserving inequality. The Left doesn't want us to be colorblind: they want us to see it all the time and think of nothing else. They want to use skin color as a means of dividing Americans from each other, just as we were divided in the days of legal segregation. But I honestly don't care what color someone's skin is, and I think most normal Americans today don't, either.

## MY FATHER'S SON

I am the son of my father, and though I took a career path different from his, I absorbed his core values. After I finished high school, while preparing to enter Fordham University in the Bronx, I signed up for Marine Officer Candidates School. My father and his brothers were all Marines. When I asked my father why he had joined the Marines, he told me, "I wanted to be with the best." That sounded like a reasonable goal and one that I wanted to follow, too.

My father was a lieutenant in the Marines and served in Vietnam as an artillery forward observer, eventually ending his career as a full colonel. He talks about it, but doesn't go into detail about combat. I sort of knew, intuitively, not to ask him if he ever killed anybody. The radio host Howard Stern once asked him on the air, not without charm, how many people he had killed. My father kind of laughed it off, which is how men of his generation usually respond to that type of thing.

We would hear stories, of course, and they were crazy, just as war is. War—as I would find out for myself—is random, wild, boring, weird, hilarious, terrifying, surreal. All kinds of stuff happens, and sometimes the only thing you can do is shrug and realize you are caught up in something so much bigger than yourself that there's no option but to roll with it.

Marine Officer Candidates School required me to attend summer boot camp sessions in Quantico, Virginia, that were excruciating and brutal. My upbringing at home wasn't especially strict; my father was hardly the Great Santini, if you're familiar with that book or movie. Arriving at OCS, on the other hand, was a definite culture shock, and adjusting to the rigors of military life was not at all natural, at least for me. I wish I could say that the boot camp experience changed me in a permanent way and made me ultra-disciplined, but once no one's yelling at you and you don't need to hop to, you pretty much go back to being your regular self.

My military service started right after the Gulf War ended, and the armed forces were resetting themselves to deal with the "New World Order" following the collapse of the Soviet Union. It's hard to believe how much the world has changed since then, and the extent to which the position of the United States has declined. It was in the Clinton years that we gave China most-favored-nation trading status, which seen from now was like committing national suicide, because they have taken over our manufacturing base—the source of our broad middle class and our national prosperity—and stolen our technological and military know-how. What a disaster:

we basically ceded our global dominance in exchange for keeping prices low on consumer electronics.

My active duty started in October 1991, when I entered training as a second lieutenant. My *Full Metal Jacket*–style basic training was mostly taken care of during the summers in college, and my entry training, while intense, was more gentlemanly. It was kind of like becoming a junior executive. Learning the trade of arms, weapons training, management training. Learning everything you need to know to lead troops into battle. They had already screened us to determine that we had what it takes to be a Marine; now they were training us to do the job of being an infantry officer, which is how all Marine officers start off. I was with about 150 other second lieutenants, and for six months there was a lot of work with weapons, going into the field, sleeping overnight, simulated battles.

When people think about the Marines, they may think about a band of brothers and team building and camaraderie. There was plenty of that, and there is no question that the average Marine is a cut above his or her civilian counterpart. But people serving in uniform are still just people. I have seen great Marines and I have seen Marines convicted of serious crimes. My time in the military has given me enormous respect for those who serve, but at the same time inoculated me against reflexively assuming that anyone in uniform is above criticism. For example, one thing that sticks out from my junior officer training was a system of peer evaluation. Everybody in the platoon—fifty guys—had to choose the top five guys and the bottom five guys. I assumed that everybody would agree on who the top and bottom people were, but I was fascinated to see that I was wrong. I was shocked to discover that only two or three men out of the entire company were not selected at all: everybody thought that somebody was either really good or really bad.

It was an unpleasant experience. They would read you the comments that other people had made about you, good and bad. It was tough to listen to, but what it really taught me was how subjective everyone's perspective can be.

My dad maintains a kind of good, simple reverence toward the Marine Corps. He'll tell you about different lessons he learned about leadership, and says that the Marines taught him how to lead. To this day, he and I can both recite the Marine Corps' fourteen Leadership Traits—justice, judgment, dependability, integrity, decisiveness, tact, initiative, endurance, bearing, unselfishness, courage, knowledge, loyalty, and enthusiasm—and maybe I don't give my service enough credit in how it's shaped me.

One thing I did learn is the importance of keeping your wits about you when all hell is breaking loose. Nothing communicates failure more than when the leader is frazzled. Also—and this sounds silly—but a leader should look like a leader. Keep your hair cut; dress the part. People who are putting their trust in you want to read the signs of self-confidence. Be decisive. Even if you make the wrong decision, that's better than making no decision. At least you will learn what doesn't work. These are things that I did learn in the Marine Corps that I have kept with me through today.

When I went back to Iraq as a journalist covering the invasion in 2003, many of these lessons came back to me. It's easy in a war zone to become an animal and let your beard grow and let your morals slip. But I made sure, even when we were sleeping in our vehicles and eating on the ground, to maintain certain key elements of propriety.

One time, someone gave me a gold-plated Walther PPK pistol that had belonged to Saddam Hussein. I said thanks, and someone else asked what I was going to do with it.

"Well," I answered, "I'm going to go throw it in the Tigris River."

"What?!?" he exclaimed. "Why? It's so cool!"

"Well, I'm not going to go over to the palace and return it, because it's dangerous," I explained. "And I'm not going to keep it, because it's illegal."

Later it got back to me that word got around that Greg Kelly is a real leader, that I set a good example—at least in war. That, I believe, came from my Marine Corps training.

I had the privilege of becoming a pilot in the Marines. I flew attack planes—the Harrier Jump Jets that you may have seen, which can take off and land vertically, like a helicopter. Being an attack jet pilot in the Marines, on board a ship for months at a time, is an amazingly intense experience. For one thing, of course, flying these intricate machines is a high-pressure, high-adrenaline activity, especially in a combat zone. Being aboard ship with thousands of other people was also a unique, and often unpleasant, experience.

I flew over Iraq when it was technically hostile territory. After the Gulf War in 1991, when we expelled Saddam's forces from Kuwait, we established a "no-fly zone" over much of Iraq throughout the nineties, as part of our sanctions regime. The United States had destroyed most of the Iraqi economy and its armed forces already. But we would control and patrol the airspace over Iraq. These flights would be recorded as combat missions, even though I was never actually fired upon and the missions became somewhat routine.

My experience deploying to the Middle East as a U.S. Marine probably enhanced my patriotism, but it also made me critical of some aspects of American foreign policy. After the terrorist attacks of September 11, 2001, when the George W. Bush administration began beating the drums for a new war against Iraq on the grounds that Saddam had developed "weapons of mass destruction," I was immediately suspicious. Having served over there, I knew full well that we had maintained total air superiority over Iraq for more than a decade. Our sanctions against the country meant that not much got in or out without our knowledge and approval. So the odds that Iraq, which could barely feed itself, had built up a sophisticated arms program without our notice seemed pretty unlikely. I don't want to come off like a foreign policy smart aleck, but I was pretty skeptical about the claims that Iraq had developed WMDs and dismayed that there weren't more voices in opposition to the war.

Domestic politics have changed a lot since the days of the Cold War. People used to think that conservatives were pro-war and liberals wanted peace. These stereotypes never really held up, of course. All the big wars in the twentieth century were started by Democrats, and it was Republicans like Dwight Eisenhower and Richard Nixon who ended the Korean and Vietnam Wars, respectively. Ronald Reagan built up our military in order to face down the Soviet threat, but he was hardly the warmonger the liberals painted him as.

I never felt comfortable with the political lines along foreign affairs in our country until Donald Trump encouraged us to put America first. I'm no fool—I believe America needs a strong military. But the occupations of Iraq and Afghanistan were a total disaster. We can't go around the world trying to impose our versions of democratic institutions and civil society on countries with completely different histories and values. It's insane.

## GROWING UP

After leaving the Marines I decided to go into broadcast journalism. I thought about law enforcement, but I wasn't sure I wanted to follow my father's career. I wanted to make my own path. I got a job in upstate New York at a regional station in Binghamton and worked hard until I got hired in New York City as a political reporter at NY1.

On 9/11, I was home in my midtown studio apartment when the planes hit. I and a cameraman were sent by the station to Beekman Downtown Hospital, a few blocks east of the World Trade Center, to report on casualties. In what emerged as a grim and gruesome footnote to that tragic day, hospitals across the city prepared for an influx of trauma cases that never came in. For the most part, people either got away from the attack, or they died.

When we saw that there wasn't much going on at the hospital, I decided to see if we could get over to the WTC site itself. National Guardsmen had blocked off the streets and wouldn't let us through, but I kept trying until one young soldier looked at my official press pass and waved us through. Press passes in New York City at that time were issued by the police department and stamped "NYPD," though local cops know very well that reporters' access to crime scenes is limited.

In any event, we got through and walked down to Church Street, right across from where the towers had stood until just a few hours earlier. It was incredibly eerie. I remember seeing a woman's high-heeled shoe in the middle of the street. A deserted fire truck covered with ash. Building 7, to the north, was still standing. I called my producer.

"We're here," I said.

"Where?"

"Down at the site . . . at the World Trade Center."

"That's impossible!" he insisted.

"I'm telling you, I'm right here in the middle of it . . . at ground zero."

I'm not 100 percent certain, but I think that was the first use of the term "ground zero" to describe the site of the biggest act of mass murder on American soil. Shortly after that, the station used it in a graphic, and pretty soon it became the standard term.

The 9/11 attacks were a revelation for everyone, and woke us up from the fantasy that the United States could rule the world from a position of splendid isolation. The world would change dramatically after that.

September 11th was also primary election day in New York City. Rudy Giuliani was term-limited and could not run for reelection. Liberal candidate Mark Green was considered the likely next mayor. He won the Democrat primary when it was finally held two weeks later, and faced Michael Bloomberg, the billionaire financial media magnate. Though Green was considered the favorite, the attack on our nation gave Giuliani the spotlight and he stood up and demonstrated real leadership. My father, like Giuliani, was backing Bloomberg, whom he considered the best man for the job. Bloomberg won and appointed my father as NYPD commissioner. Having first served under Mayor Dinkins in the early nineties, my dad was the first person ever to fill the position of NYPD commissoner twice.

I was hired by Fox News in late 2002, and Roger Ailes asked me if I would be willing to go to Iraq. Having been there before, I said sure, but I didn't really believe the invasion would happen. I was assigned to Atlanta, but before I could even find an apartment, Fox News management told me they wanted me to go over to Kuwait. Looking back, I was sort of blasé about the whole thing. Other reporters were constantly marveling at the vast military apparatus, and filing stories on MREs (Meals, Ready to Eat, the boxed field rations the Army distributes to soldiers), while to me it was just chow.

I had left the Marines only a few years before, so a lot of the experiences were familiar to me. This caused some friction with the public affairs officers who were assigned to manage the media, because it was harder to wow me with flak jackets and military nomenclature than some of the other reporters who had experienced only civilian life.

I was embedded with the Third Infantry Division, Second Brigade Combat team, which was like the headquarters element of a big tank brigade, with three tank battalions. We had live satellite coverage and were rolling live as we crossed the border into Iraq. Quite frankly, it was a thrilling experience. I was the first television reporter to broadcast live images of our forces reaching the presidential palace in Baghdad. It was heady stuff.

I would return to Iraq several times over the next few years, each time feeling increasingly vindicated that my initial doubts about the reasons for the war had been correct. I was later assigned to cover the White House and the Pentagon, but given my position on the war and who I was ideologically at the time, it was an uneasy fit politically for me within Fox.

Subsequently, I transferred inside Fox to host *Good Day New York* for almost ten years. Those were good years. I should note that a brush with law enforcement came during that period, in 2012, when a woman I had met went to the police and claimed I had raped her. The NYPD, which was run by my father at the time, recused itself from the investigation and turned the case over to the Manhattan district attorney, whose office maintains the nation's foremost sex crime investigation unit. The DA examined the case in depth for two weeks and issued a letter stating that the facts did not indicate any violation of the law. *The Huffington Post* described the letter as a "total exoneration."

Because of my local fame and who my father was, the case was national headline news. It is no exaggeration to say that the story received considerably more press attention than Tara Reade's accusation of sexual assault against Joe Biden did a few years later. I was thankful that the system worked, and thoroughly exonerated me, but I got a taste of what it's like to be in the spotlight of scandal, which is a thoroughly traumatizing experience.

## REAL NEWS AND FAKE NEWS

I've made my career in broadcast journalism for over twenty years now, and consider myself a serious student of the form. The lying, cowardice, and partisanship of my colleagues in this industry regarding Trump and his policies have never been seen before in American history.

Part of the reason I wanted to write this book is that the lying media—the "fake news"—has put our country in danger. There has always been a "slant" to the news, but Trump's presidency caused the American Left to go insane and drop everything they pretended to know about fairness and honesty. The explosion in crime across the country goes unremarked upon or excused because to mention it would give ammunition to Trump and his supporters. Everything in American life is now cast in terms of whether it would help or hurt Trump.

I make my living in the news media, but I don't consider myself part of the beast. Reporters and media figures used to at least pretend to report the news in an unbiased, nonpartisan manner. A careful listener or reader knew there was underlying bias, but journalists at least attempted to keep their personal opinions buried. Neutrality was still the standard by which the game was played.

That's all gone. The mainstream media is now avowedly far to the Left. They all went along with the Democrat lies about Russia-gate and Trump, they pushed the treason narrative, they amplified leftist lies about the police, and they colluded to keep the American people in the dark about essential matters.

Law and order have deteriorated badly in America over the last decade. The American way of life is under ruthless, relentless attack. If we don't act, and act fast, to roll back the damage, the country we know and love will be gone for good.

# CHAPTER ONE

## Defunding the Police or Defending the Police

THE DEATH OF GEORGE FLOYD at the end of May 2020 provoked a kind of mass hysteria across America. Locked down, quarantined, driven crazy by four years of media madness about Donald Trump and his allegedly racist and authoritarian regime, people in cities across the country saw the infamous video of Minneapolis police officer Derek Chauvin kneeling on the neck of career criminal, aspiring porn star, and drug addict George Floyd, and went into a collective temper tantrum.

America erupted. Protests attracted millions of people who marched with banners declaring that "Black Lives Matter" and demanding—in a unified voice, seemingly out of nowhere—that police departments across the country be "defunded" and disbanded.

City after city burned. Minneapolis and St. Paul were rocked by violent protests that resulted in widespread looting and arson, which caused massive destruction to property. Blocks of businesses were set ablaze. The Minneapolis Police Department's Third Precinct building was besieged by thousands of protestors and began receiving mortar fire. Thirteen officers, grossly outnumbered, huddled inside and sent text messages to their families in anticipation of being killed. As the protestors breached the station, Mayor Jacob Frey gave the order to evacuate and abandon the building, which was invaded and burned by a gleeful mob.

The scene was repeated across the nation. While the country remained "locked down" because of COVID-19—with schools, gyms, and churches closed for fear of catching a virus that turned out to be dangerous mostly for people over eighty-five—massive protests were exempted from the general prohibition on the grounds that "the public health risks of not protesting to demand an end to systemic racism greatly exceed the harms of the virus," as one Johns Hopkins epidemiologist said in an utterly preposterous claim.[1] Outdoor church services with parishioners seated far apart from each other were broken up by the police,[2] but enormous marches and rallies demanding an end to policing were celebrated as a necessary antidote to "structural racism."

Anarchist protestors in Portland, Oregon, began a three-month series of nightly demonstrations, most of which were declared unlawful riots. "Antifascist" terrorists known as Antifa, dressed all in black, wearing masks, and carrying shields and batons, deployed urban warfare tactics to destroy property, attack cops, and commit arson. Close to two-thirds of all Portland protests were classified as "violent."[3] Efforts were made to burn down the Multnomah County Justice Center and to destroy federal property; protestors used powerful handheld lasers to damage the eyesight of more than one hundred federal officers.

In Seattle, a mob declared the Capitol Hill neighborhood an "Autonomous Zone" and barricaded the streets to prevent police or emergency service vehicles from entering. Neighborhood businesses were looted, residents were terrorized, and two people were murdered before the city managed to resume policing the area after three weeks.

In New York, thousands of protestors blocked streets and attacked police, hundreds of whom were injured. Two lawyers were arrested for bombing a police car; they also distributed Molotov cocktails and planned to attack NYPD headquarters. Urooj Rahman and Colinford Mattis pleaded guilty to federal charges of conspiracy to commit arson; originally facing decades in prison, the Biden Department of Justice is seeking a slap on the wrist of these two would-be terrorists. Businesses across the city boarded up their front windows to prevent looting and destruction. A "protestor" placed a megaphone against a cop's ear and screamed into it, causing permanent damage to her hearing.

It didn't end there. Across the nation, thousands of police were injured in the protests, as rioters attacked them with bricks, frozen water bottles, fireworks, and even Molotov cocktails. At least one hundred police vehicles were burned. Aside from the intense weeks of protests following George Floyd's death, over 60,000 law enforcement officers were assaulted throughout 2020, versus only 4,071 the year before.[4] One-third of those cops sustained injuries. And though thousands of violent rioters were arrested, more than half of them had their charges dropped by leftist pro-chaos prosecutors.

Some rioters profited handsomely from their misbehavior. An Austin, Texas, man who was participating in anti-police violence was struck in the head by a beanbag round fired by the police, a nonlethal defensive measure sometimes employed during riots. The city settled a lawsuit, awarding him a whopping $8 million. Furthermore, nineteen Austin police officers were indicted on charges of using "excessive force." They may lose their jobs and go to jail for defending themselves and their city from the rampages of a violent mob.[5]

## MOB RULE

This urban street chaos wasn't unprecedented. America had experienced civil unrest driven by anger over policing before. In the 1960s, race riots in major cities resulted in substantial death and damage—in fact, far more than we saw following the George Floyd riots. The 1965 Watts riots in Los Angeles erupted after cops stopped a black drunk driver who resisted arrest: the weeklong riot resulted in thirty-four deaths and significant property damage.

A police raid on an unlicensed Detroit bar in 1967 led to a week of severe unrest, with forty-three deaths, including civilians, law enforcement, and firefighters. Snipers and National Guardsmen engaged in open gun battles with each other, and hundreds of buildings were burned to the ground. A race riot over the beating of a black motorist by Newark, New Jersey, police during the same "long, hot summer" resulted in more than two dozen deaths.

After the assassination of Martin Luther King Jr. in April 1968, the nation's major cities were rocked by riots. Washington, D.C., experienced heavy looting and arson, and the city suffered catastrophic economic losses that weren't recouped for another twenty-five years. Baltimore and Chicago were put under martial law; Mayor Richard J. Daley of Chicago told his cops to "shoot to kill" arsonists and "shoot to maim" looters.

In 1980, Miami erupted after the acquittal of four police officers accused of killing a black motorist; eighteen people died in the ensuing days of rage. The 1992 riots in Los Angeles were precipitated by the acquittal of four Los Angeles Police Department officers who had been videotaped seriously beating Rodney King, a black man who had led the cops on a high-speed chase. More than sixty people were killed and considerable property damage was sustained, especially in Koreatown, where thousands of businesses were looted and destroyed.

The bloodshed of the riots of the past was more intense than what we have seen recently, largely because police and National Guardsmen are much less likely to shoot at rioters than they used to be. But there was one other major difference between the George Floyd riots of 2020 and the disorder of decades ago. During earlier riots, the media and almost all politicians saw what was happening and commented on it accurately. Newspapers and television reported what they saw and didn't sugarcoat it with pretty words about the gallantry of the rioters. And politicians and other major figures universally denounced the violence, though they may have disagreed about its causes.

## MAKING EXCUSES

Following the 1967 riots, President Lyndon Johnson appointed a blue-ribbon commission led by Otto Kerner Jr., the governor of Illinois, to investigate the causes of the disorder. Kerner, a New Deal–style Chicago liberal (who was later convicted of mail fraud in a racetrack bribery scandal), and his commission found that inner-city rioting happened because "our Nation is moving toward two societies, one black, one white—separate and unequal."

The Kerner Commission—whose report became a nationwide bestseller when it was published in March 1968—concluded that structural racism in the form of "segregation and poverty" had created "in the racial ghetto a destructive environment totally unknown to most white Americans." It blamed "white racism" for the "explosive mixture which has been accumulating in our cities since the end of World War II."[6]

The main solution was to enact "new taxes" in order to achieve "unprecedented levels of funding" to pay for "new initiatives and experiments that can change the system of failure and frustration that now dominates the ghetto and weakens our society."

The enormous outlays of LBJ's Great Society programs—Medicaid, Medicare, the expansion of Social Security and food stamps, the Elementary and Secondary Education Act, Head Start, Job Corps, etc.—which radically and rapidly grew the scope of the federal government, and have accounted for tens of trillions of dollars of spending and the transformation of America into a kind of social democratic welfare state, were dismissed as insufficient. New, massive programs would have to be developed if we were to really target the "root causes" of violence.

But the immediate problem identified by the Kerner Commission as the cause of urban rioting was community hostility to the police, whom they regarded as an "occupying force." The report explained that

> [t]he policeman in the ghetto is a symbol not only of law, but of the entire system of law enforcement and criminal justice. As such, he becomes the tangible target for grievances against shortcomings throughout that system: Against assembly-line justice in teeming lower courts; against wide disparities in sentences; against antiquated correctional facilities; against the basic inequities imposed by the system on the poor—to whom, for example, the option of bail means only jail.

Does this sound familiar? I bet it does, if you've been paying even the slightest attention to the narrative that has been blasted by the mainstream media 24/7 since George Floyd died. All the complaints about the police that we hear today—that cops "hunt" black people for sport or that the police are the descendants of "slave catchers"—have their roots in liberal rhetoric from the sixties. Today we have the same bad actors and peddlers of division who are busily selling the poison.

Of course there has been racism in America, and it was certainly worse fifty or sixty years ago. But the amazing thing about Americans—I mean regular people, not politicians, academics, or *Morning Joe* panelists—is how successfully we have faced our social problems and overcome them. Despite what the race hustlers and far-left media try to beat into us, America is a place where anyone of any color or creed can succeed on his or her own merits.

And if you are short on natural talent . . . well, hard work counts for a lot, and can paper over all kinds of other deficits.

At the same time, it would be foolish to pretend that there was never any racism or race-based police brutality in America. There was. But it's worth pointing out that even the ultraliberal Kerner Commission was skeptical about how much actual police violence—as opposed to popular perception and rumors—was to blame for the 1967 riots.

The commission dug deep into the facts of the riots and their precipitating factors. What set everything off? Did racist cops pummel a little kid for no reason? Did they see an old lady drop a candy wrapper and decide to deliver some kneecap justice?

Actually, no. In Newark, Detroit, New York, and other cities, the "disturbances studied by the Commission began with a police incident. But these incidents were not, for the most part, the crude acts of an earlier time. They were routine police actions such as stopping a motorist or raiding an illegal business." In every case, the cops effected a normal arrest of someone who had done something objectively illegal, and there's no evidence—or even contemporary allegations—that the police were acting abusively.

So what caused the riots? Human beings are imitative and reactive by nature. As the summer of 1967—oddly enough, famous as both the "Summer of Love" and the "Long, Hot Summer"—wore on, cities caught fire in succession, as if the locals decided, *What the hell, let's jump in, too.* In this tinderbox environment, it didn't take much to set things off.

## COLORBLIND?

Of course, the definition of police brutality can be subjective. The Kerner Report makes the curious point that the same actions, in different neighborhoods, will have different effects. "Many officers simply fail to understand the effects of their actions because of their limited knowledge of the Negro community. . . . A patrolman may take the arm of a person he is leading to the police car. Negroes are more likely to resent this than whites because the action implies that they are on the verge of flight and may degrade them in the eyes of friends or onlookers."

In other words, the cops in 1967 didn't understand that they had to treat black suspects more tenderly than they would white suspects, because the black suspects would take offense to being treated like criminals . . . even if that was what they were. It's weird to think that just fifty-five years ago we were being told that treating different people the same way was a form of racism.

When I was growing up and, later, serving my country in the military, I was always taught that the key to equality and getting along is—as Martin Luther King Jr. said—to judge everyone according to the content of their character, not the color of their skin. Treating different people differently, I learned, was the essence of racism.

Today we are being told the opposite. Being "colorblind" is just a way for whites to avoid dealing with their own racism. Instead of being colorblind, we are supposed to see color all the time, and nothing but color.

It used to be racist to treat different people differently. But now it's considered racist to want to treat everyone the same. Acting as though black and white people are equals, according to the new way of thinking about race, just preserves the deep imbalances that persist in our society, which is shot through with racism. According to this theory, the only way to undo centuries of racism is through more racism. Treating whites and blacks by different standards will, given enough time, help us achieve the equality that we have always talked about.

If this sounds crazy to you, you aren't alone. To listen to today's activists, you'd think that the last sixty years—the Civil Rights Act, desegregation, trillions of dollars in wealth transfer—never happened. We are stuck eternally in the era of Jim Crow, which, according to President Biden, hasn't ended. In fact, he believes, it is turning into "Jim Eagle" in states under Republican control.[7]

Back in the real world, of course, that fantasy of entrenched racism doesn't relate to reality. We live in a country where black people appear at the polls at a greater rate than white people—when they want to. In 2008 and 2012, when Barack Obama was on the ballot, black voter turnout was between four and six points higher than white turnout. In 2020, black women and white men voted at exactly the same rate. There is no bar to voting in America except motivation.[8]

Anyway, the idea that we live in a country where the choice today, as Biden says, is being "on the side of Dr. King or George Wallace? Do you want to be on the side of John Lewis or Bull Connor? Do you want to be on the side of Abraham Lincoln or Jefferson Davis?" is offensive and absurd.[9] I suspect a lot of the people listening to Biden didn't know who Bull Connor (a lifelong Democrat who was born in 1897) even was. But think about who's speaking: Joe Biden, who was born before D-Day, and counted among his closest friends in the Senate hard-core segregationists like James Eastland and Strom Thurmond.[10]

Sometimes it feels like liberals enjoy pretending that people who are fifty or sixty years old are former Klansmen who grew up in the days when it was normal to have segregated drinking fountains, or to make black people stand up on the bus when a white person wanted to sit down. But your average sixty-year-old white man today was an infant when JFK was killed, listened to Donna Summer in high school, and was in his twenties when Michael Jordan won his first NBA championship. It's one thing to acknowledge the importance of history and the past. But you have to at least admit that it's in the past.

## SEEING REALITY

The massive riots of 1967—and the ones that followed in the decades to come—were universally seen, discussed, and interpreted as riots. There were arguments about the "root causes." There was debate about what to do to prevent future riots. But almost nobody except for some communist professors pretended that the riots were legitimate expressions of political opinion. America had a shared comprehension of what had happened: people burned down buildings, attacked the police, looted stores, and got killed, and this was *wrong*.

Contrast that to the way Democrats and the Left registered the 2020 George Floyd riots, which a CNN graphic praised as "mostly peaceful," even as fires raged on camera and we watched as Kenosha, Wisconsin, burned—and for those of you who can't keep track, I'm talking about the first time Kenosha burned, during the Floyd riots. ("K-Town" burned again a few months later, after the police shot and wounded Jacob Blake, an armed domestic abuser.)

Beginning in early June, as Minneapolis and then other cities faced rioting and arson, the mainstream media and leading Democrat politicians went into denial mode; insisting that you should ignore the evidence of your two lying eyes, and instead absorb and believe the narrative that they pumped straight into the American consciousness, without regard for fact. Thus began one of the most shameful episodes in American public life, as the elites engaged in a war on the truth, blaming the police and an innocent public for the collapse in public order and the destruction of our urban centers.

News from the first few days after George Floyd's death in

Minneapolis was relatively straightforward and fact-based. Media reports described the chaos, violence, and arson more or less as it was, in the manner of how news organizations are trusted to act.

But then, on the night of May 28, everything changed. President Trump tweeted, in response to the chaos unfolding in Minneapolis, that he expected the police to take charge of the situation, which was spiraling out of control.

> I can't stand back & watch this happen to a great American City, Minneapolis. A total lack of leadership. Either the very weak Radical Left Mayor, Jacob Frey, get his act together and bring the City under control, or I will send in the National Guard & get the job done right. . . .

> . . . These THUGS are dishonoring the memory of George Floyd, and I won't let that happen. Just spoke to Governor Tim Walz and told him that the Military is with him all the way. Any difficulty and we will assume control but, when the looting starts, the shooting starts. Thank you!

Trump's comment about looting and shooting is ambiguous. On one hand, it means that mass looting and robbery is typically a prelude to greater mob violence; on the other, it is a threat that the police will step in and clean things up if the unrest doesn't end. "Looting leads to shooting, and that's why a man was shot and killed in Minneapolis on Wednesday night," the president tweeted the next day. "Or look at what just happened in Louisville with 7 people shot. I don't want this to happen, and that's what the expression put out last night means." He said later that he meant it as both a statement of fact and as an admonishment.

The press and Democrat leaders worked up a frenzy over

Trump's remarks. Chicago mayor Lori Lightfoot blamed Trump for the protests and violence that were beginning to spread throughout the Loop. "I will code what I want to say and it starts with *F* and ends with *U*," she told assembled media. "The president is fomenting violence. There is no other way to read that tweet.

"We see the game he's playing because it's so transparent and he's not very good at it," Lightfoot continued. "He wants to show failures on the part of Democratic local leaders . . . [H]is goal is to polarize, to destabilize local government and to inflame racist urges. And we can absolutely not let him prevail." Mayor Lightfoot insisted that "being black in America should not be a death sentence." The implication of her remarks was that black people are being put to death for no reason, and that Donald Trump was to blame.

Within a day of her comments, the "Magnificent Mile" had been looted, multiple people had been shot and killed by "protestors," dozens of cops had been injured, drawbridges over the Chicago River had been raised in order to prevent mobs from destroying the Loop, and Mayor Lightfoot had implored Illinois governor J. B. Pritzker to call out the National Guard to restore order, for the first time in more than half a century. Blocked from looting big-name downtown luxury stores, rioters turned to their neighborhood businesses. Pharmacies were stripped bare. Trucks backed through storefronts in order to facilitate mass stealing.

On May 31, eighteen people, mostly black, were killed in Chicago—not by the police, but by local criminals and rioters. Calls to 911, normally totaling about 15,000 a day, soared to 65,000. Most went unanswered as police, overwhelmed, desperately tried to maintain order.

Keisha Lance Bottoms, the mayor of Atlanta, similarly confused cause and effect, blaming Trump for the escalating rioting and violence rocking the Big Peach. "He should just stop talking," Bottoms told CNN. "He speaks and he makes it worse. There are times when you should just be quiet and I wish that he would just be quiet. Or if he can't be silent, if there is somebody of good sense and good conscience in the White House, put him in front of a teleprompter and pray he reads it and at least says the right things, because he is making it worse."

Liberal politicians and media were creating yet another false narrative: that Trump's tweets sparked the violence. But you must remember that well before his tweet, Atlanta mobs attacked police, burned police cars, looted the College Football Hall of Fame, and tried to burn down the CNN headquarters. Hundreds of protestors were arrested over the next several weeks, and the National Guard was called out to enforce a curfew.

## ATTACK ON THE WHITE HOUSE

In Washington, D.C., hundreds of protestors attempted to storm the White House. They crossed barricades near the Treasury Department, getting within one hundred yards of the East Wing. Sixty Secret Service agents were injured, and President Trump and his family were briefly moved to a secure underground bunker, which late-night TV comedians perversely found hilarious.

Riots, fires, and looting broke out across the District, including at St. John's Church, a historic house of worship one block from the White House. Since 1816, every president has attended services at St. John's. Thousands of protestors took over Lafayette Square, across the street from the White House. Every night, anarchist rioters tried to overrun Secret Service barricades around the president's home, but were repelled with tear gas and pepper bullets.

Wanting to show the country that the nation's capital was not controlled by the mob, President Trump went to St. John's Church to give a press conference. The howling mob of rioters and protestors outside the White House began throwing "bricks, frozen water bottles, and caustic liquids" at the United States Park Police.

After a warning, the mob was cleared by the Park Police, who used smoke, loud flashes, and mounted officers. Trump spoke briefly while holding a Bible, then visited the church.

For some reason, this act was described as especially despicable. Joe Biden, presumptive Democratic nominee, said, "When peaceful protesters are dispersed by the order of the president from the door-step of the people's house, the White House—using tear gas and flash grenades—in order to stage a photo op at a noble church, we can be forgiven for believing that the president is more interested in power than in principle." Senator Kamala Harris condemned the sight of "President Trump, having gassed peaceful protesters just so he could do this photo op, then he went on to tear-gas priests who were helping protesters in Lafayette Park." House Speaker Nancy Pelosi said it was characteristic of a "banana republic."

And how so? Just what is so offensive about holding a Bible out-side a church? It's ludicrous that a Bible is a corrupt symbol, while hoisting the "Black Lives Matter" emblem above the same church was later held to be beautiful and appropriate.

The press swallowed this message, reporting thousands of times, uncritically, that President Trump had violently cleared peaceful protestors so he could stage a "photo op." Many repeated the canard that Trump had violated the constitutional rights of the protestors. Lawrence O'Donnell, an MSNBC host, commented:

> You would think that if you had not seen how [Attorney General] William Barr and Donald Trump treated this church in Washington, D.C., across from the White House as just a backdrop for a photo op which was condemned by the pastor of that church, it was condemned by the bishop of that church and was only made possible because Donald Trump and William Barr used tear gas on American citizens exercising their First Amendment right to protest in that location that Donald Trump wanted to use it as a photo op.

The fact that the priest and bishop of a church that had been set on fire were hesitant to criticize the people who set the fire is more a measure of their own terror and fear of retribution than a statement of the justice of arson. But it's also interesting that the press and leading Democrat politicians criticized Trump for "staging a photo op" and imposing a security perimeter to do so.

Anytime elected officials do anything in public it's a photo op. That's their whole political existence. There's literally no time that a president goes outside in front of people that he isn't doing it in order to be photographed. The fact that the Secret Service clears the way for a sitting president is no surprise. There are always people who want to protest in front of the president; it doesn't matter how peaceful they are or aren't—they will be told to move, and if they refuse, they will necessarily be pushed away.

Consider the inauguration of Joe Biden. Two weeks before he became president, the January 6, 2021, riot at the Capitol briefly disrupted the operations of Congress. Protestors occupied the Capitol for a few hours before dispersing. There was no significant damage done to the historic building. No members of Congress were injured. Congress resumed its joint session that same evening and confirmed Biden's Electoral College victory.

For Biden's inauguration ceremony, Washington, D.C., was placed under martial law. Riot fencing controlled movement throughout the city. Twenty-five thousand troops were called to occupy the capital, a military presence that hadn't been seen in the District since the Civil War. The National Mall, traditionally open to the public on a nonticketed basis so people can watch the inauguration in person, was sealed. Most of downtown Washington was closed off. The mayor asked tourists not to visit, and Airbnb canceled all reservations. All regional rail service was suspended. The postceremony motorcade and parade from the Capitol to the White House—the same route that Trump had walked four years before, in front of hundreds of thousands of people—was empty except for lines of troops.

Nobody in the press complained that President Biden was a fascist or tinpot dictator staging security theater, terrorizing the city, and preventing peaceful protestors from exercising their First Amendment rights.

Incidentally, constitutionally protected protest under the First Amendment includes the right of peaceful assembly, speech, and the redress of grievances. Occupying streets in violation of a police order is not constitutionally protected. This is a major misunderstanding on the part of the Left, which confuses the moral legitimacy that civil disobedience in service of a righteous cause might have, with First Amendment protest. The point of civil disobedience is that protestors intentionally break the law and indicate that they are willing to be punished in order to show that another law is unjust.

But people camping in a public park, breaking windows, setting fires, and violating curfew are breaking the law. They may or may not be practicing civil disobedience, but they shouldn't expect to have constitutional protection for their actions. Former CNN anchor Chris Cuomo personified this confusion. "Too many see the protests as the problem," he counseled. "No, the problem is what forced your fellow citizens to take to the streets. Persistent and poisonous inequities and injustice. And please, show me where it says that protests are supposed to be polite and peaceful." Well, the text of the First Amendment is a good place to start: "Congress shall make no law . . . abridging the freedom of speech, or of the press; or the right of the people *peaceably* to assemble. . . . "

## MOSTLY PEACEFUL

Cuomo made his preposterously stupid comment the same day that Trump went across the street to visit St. John's Church. It was around this time that the press adopted the bizarre and Orwellian phrase "mostly peaceful protests." A mob of two thousand people might mill around until nightfall, and then three hundred of them could set fires, attack the police with rocks and shine powerful lasers in their eyes, and try to blow up security fencing with improvised mortars, and reporters would contend that the event was "mostly peaceful."

The first widely noted example of this abuse of language came on May 28, 2020, when Ali Velshi, an MSNBC contributor, reported from Minneapolis in front of burning buildings. "I want to be clear in how I characterize this," he explained. "This is mostly a protest. It is not, generally speaking, unruly, but fires have been started."

The most famous example happened a few months later, after Jacob Blake was shot in Kenosha, Wisconsin. Blake's estranged girl-friend had called 911 and reported that he had shown up at her house, even though she had a restraining order against him, and sto-len her car keys and was refusing to give them back. The police were informed that Blake, who is black, had an outstanding warrant for charges of sexual assault and disorderly conduct. Blake resisted arrest, was Tased twice to no effect, and then reached inside his girlfriend's car to grab a knife. The police then shot Blake, who was wounded.

The city of Kenosha exploded in violent protests. Forty commer-cial buildings were completely destroyed by fire, and an additional hundred properties were damaged. A CNN reporter stood in front of what he described as "multiple locations" set aflame across the city. Behind him, a massive fire engulfed a block of buildings, and burnt-out cars loomed in what looked like an apocalyptic disaster scene. As the reporter described the scene, the text in front of him read, FIERY BUT MOSTLY PEACEFUL PROTESTS AFTER POLICE SHOOTING.

If it weren't so tragic you'd want to laugh, and if it weren't so funny you'd want to cry. Yes, indeed, many episodes of intense vio-lence involve breathing periods. The Manson Family wasn't always killing people, but you wouldn't want to call them a "mostly peace-ful" death cult. During World War I, trench warfare involved long periods of boredom punctuated by terrifying artillery barrages, but you wouldn't characterize the millions of deaths as occurring during a "mostly peaceful" war, except for a few interruptions.

The press narrative around the 2020 riots was married to the idea that the violence was all incidental. It happened adjacent to the protests, which were essentially civil and orderly. Perhaps the violence was caused by agitators, or a few bad eggs. Maybe it was "incited" by police repression, or by President Trump's intemperate tweets. Or maybe it didn't really matter very much, because, as people liked to say, quoting Martin Luther King, "A riot is the language of the unheard." In other words, it's our fault, because when you refuse to let people speak out and have their grievances heard, it's to be expected that they will act out in extraordinary ways.

In September 2020, a nonprofit group called the Armed Conflict Location & Event Data Project (ACLED) issued a widely cited report that found that 93 percent of the year's Black Lives Matter–related protests were peaceful and nondestructive.[11] Only 7 percent were marred by violence. CNN rushed to assert that the ACLED report "contradicts assumptions and claims by some that protests associated with the Black Lives Matter movement are spawning violence and destruction of property." Two Harvard professors wrote an op-ed for the *Washington Post* insisting that "the Black Lives Matter uprisings were remarkably nonviolent." In fact, out of 7,305 documented protests in 2,400 locations over the course of three months, only 550 were found to have been violent.

Translated, that means that the country only had an average of seven violent protests a day. Is that supposed to be impressive? Or peaceful?

## BURNING THINGS FOR JUSTICE

Another, even more pernicious theme began to be voiced as looting continued and property burned. As damage from the George

Floyd riots mounted into the billions of dollars, the Left promoted a novel and deeply cynical argument: property crime—arson, looting—doesn't matter. Nikole Hannah-Jones, the brains behind the *New York Times*' hallucinatory 1619 Project, was asked to offer her opinion on the ongoing riots. "We need to be really careful with our language," Hannah-Jones admonished. "Violence is when an agent of the state kneels on a man's neck until all of the life is leached out of his body. Destroying property, which can be replaced, is not violence."[12]

The New America Foundation, a well-respected D.C. think tank run by Anne-Marie Slaughter, a former official in the Obama State Department, published an article explaining that "over the past week, a certain narrative has taken root—one that considers property damage to be a bigger problem than the continued massacre of Black people by police." This argument is built on multiple deceptions and argumentative flaws. For one thing, there is no "continued massacre" of black people by police. I get into this more in depth in another chapter, but the data on police shootings of black people who aren't armed shows that it happens maybe once a month or so, nationwide.

Furthermore, everyone agrees that life is more valuable than property. It's commonplace to say after a bad accident, "Well, at least nobody was hurt." The activists try to make a logical leap, accusing people who complain about burning buildings and looting of diminishing human life. But there is no necessary connection between saving lives—black or white—and destroying property or stealing. It's not either/or.

## DO BLACK LIVES MATTER?

When it comes to a black life that ought to have mattered to the people who claimed they care so much about them but didn't, let me say a word now about David Dorn. Dorn, a black man, was a retired St. Louis police captain. He served the Metropolitan Police

Department of St. Louis with distinction from 1969 until 2007. His body was discovered in the early hours of June 2, 2020, outside his friend's pawnshop. Dorn had responded to the burglar alarm at the store, and was shot and murdered by members of the gang of thieves who had been breaking in. They streamed his killing on Facebook. One member of the gang, Stephan Cannon, was convicted of first-degree murder in Dorn's killing.

In a society that meant what it said about the value of black lives, the news of Dorn's death would have been met with an immediate cessation of rioting and looting. Someone put a small cardboard sign at the site of the murder that summed up the whole tragic irony: "Y'all killed a black man because 'they' killed a black man??? Rest in peace." But, of course, Dorn's death did nothing to sate the mob's appetite for destruction. Things actually got worse.

The most dangerous thing about the rioting and revolutionary violence wasn't the fact that people were looting and burning and killing. That's always happened, and America has the law enforcement and National Guard to deal with it. For example, Antifa is a loose confederation of goons and losers who dress up in black to anonymize themselves when they go out in gangs to destroy things. These are poisonous thugs. They think it's fun to buy powerful laser pointers and shine them into people's eyes, hoping to destroy their retinas. Another trick they have is to put quick-drying concrete into "milk shakes" and throw them at people they don't like. They are uniformly ugly, sad scum who claim to be "antifascists" and anarchists, and who cherish the idea of murdering police officers and burning down property.

Antifa types have been around for a long time. America used to have a lot of anarchists roaming around throwing bombs and killing people. In 1901, a crazed anarchist named Leon Czolgosz shot and killed President William McKinley. In 1916, some anarchists bombed a "Preparedness Day" parade in San Francisco, killing ten people and wounding forty; the following year, nine policemen and a bystander were killed by a bomb that was left in a Milwaukee church.

The difference between the anarchist mayhem of the past and what we saw in 2020 was that political officials and members of the press didn't deny what the terror was one hundred years ago. But in 2020 we saw numerous high-ranking Democrats insist that Antifa was a myth or fantasy cooked up by fever-line conservatives overdosing on cable news coverage. Senator Kamala Harris, shortly before she was nominated for the vice presidency, tweeted out support for arrested rioters in Minneapolis on June 1, 2020, encouraging her followers, "If you're able to, chip in now to the @MNFreedomFund to help post bail for those protesting on the ground in Minnesota."[13]

The people who had been arrested for "protesting" in Minnesota weren't being rounded up by federal police on Trump's orders: they had been arrested by local police in a deep-blue city in a deep-blue state. But the need to pretend that these vicious riots were the pursuit of justice was so strong that the suffering of normal people at the hands of brutes was immaterial. Similarly, when New York congressman Jerry Nadler was asked about coordinated Antifa violence in Portland, he said that Antifa was a "myth."[14]

Even four-star generals got in on the act. Mark Milley, chairman of the Joint Chiefs of Staff, gave a sniveling apology for having accompanied Trump to stand in front of St. John's Church. After saying that his presence there "created a perception of the military involved in domestic politics," he went on to proclaim without doubt his involvement in domestic politics—on the other side. Milley seemed to excuse the lawlessness of the protests by citing the injustice of George Floyd's death. "The protests that have ensued not only speak to his killing, but also to the centuries of injustice toward African Americans," Milley said. "What we are seeing is the long shadow of our original sin in Jamestown 401 years ago, liberated by the Civil War, but not equal in the eyes of the law until 100 years later in 1965."[15]

Milley went on to condemn the existence of "implicit bias" in the military and swore to eradicate it. Implicit bias is a pseudoscientific quality that is assumed to exist subconsciously in our brains, affecting how we treat nonwhites. Testing has failed to demonstrate that it is real, or that there is anything that can be done about it if it does exist. Milley shouldn't even be talking about this ghostly entity, much less pledging to eliminate it.

The Left has no problem insisting that white supremacy is America's biggest problem right now. The fact that there is no white supremacist organization to point to isn't a problem for them. But when thousands of anarchists are known to be crossing the country and planning to blow up federal buildings in the name of Antifa, all of a sudden this violent conspiracy becomes a "tendency," an "idea."

## PROPERTY "CRIME"

Over the few years since the George Floyd riots, America has been beset by a massive shoplifting epidemic. As cities and states have ceased prosecuting theft under one thousand dollars or so, police have stopped bothering to arrest thieves. Everyone has seen videos of thieves loading up garbage bags with whatever they want from pharmacies, big-box stores, and even department stores, and walking out, knowing that the security guards have been instructed not to tangle with them. And it's common now on social media or in conversation to hear people snidely remark, "It's insured." The same thing was said during the riots, after entire commercial blocks were gutted by fire. "They have insurance, right?"

The stupidity and cynicism behind this sentiment are so profound that it speaks to a decay in our culture that is almost past understanding. Yes, life is more valuable than property, but property sustains life. There's a reason why we call someone's business or profession their "livelihood." A small business owner feeds his or her children through the work that they do. Who is so detached and removed from everyday life to imagine that just because something is insured, there is no cost to losing it?

People whose businesses were burned down across the country during the George Floyd/BLM riots are lucky if they recoup even a portion of their costs. Large national chains have had to sue their insurers over questions such as, Were the riots a single "occurrence" or many "events"? Different types of coverage return different answers. Many small businesses may have been covered for the cost of goods they lost or for rebuilding their property, but what about their lost income for a year or more as they waited to get paid and then rebuild their businesses? What about the higher cost of premiums? Or what if they can't even get new coverage?

People who sneer at the cost of property damage are completely naïve. They are the sort of people who have never built anything or known the pride of ownership. Perhaps they work for government, the nonprofit complex, or as knowledge workers who think the real world is for suckers. Ultimately, their scorn for property indicates their scorn for life as people really live it. They might even relish the thought of arson and mass looting, because they dream of destroying society and creating a communist world where no one owns anything.

Nikole Hannah-Jones said something else subtly evil in her comment about how destroying property is not violence. "Violence," she said, "is when an agent of the state kneels on a man's neck until all of the life is leached out of his body." Notice that she limits "violence" to when "an agent of the state" kills someone. It appears that leftist radicals like Hannah-Jones don't just want to see property destroyed with impunity. They don't think it's necessarily bad when people hurt or kill other people—as long as it's the right people doing it and getting it done to.

## RESTORATIVE INJUSTICE

The primary demand that grew out of the George Floyd protests was to "defund the police." All of a sudden, in every city, activists and Democrats were insisting that the police had to have their budgets slashed. According to Black Lives Matter, "There are more effective methods of providing safety and security to our communities—methods that reject the murder and brutalization of Black people." These "more effective methods" include—you guessed it—more funding for social services, mental health treatment, and "reparative justice solutions."[16]

Reparative, or "restorative," justice, in case you're not familiar, means that you sit down with the person who beat you up, he explains why he did it, you tell him how badly it hurt, and a mediator helps the two of you come up with an "action plan" to address past harms and avoid future ones. Most importantly, "rather than blaming the offender, this system considers crime as a problem to be solved collectively. With the input of the courts and the community, restitution is used fairly to deal with nearly all crimes. Major emphasis is placed on the offender's social reintegration and on a reconciliation with the crime victim."[17] "Detention" is considered a measure of last resort, and never as a means of punishment—only to prevent more harm.

But the main purpose of the Defund movement is not really to eliminate police; it's just to change who the police are and whom they answer to. Democrats just don't like the idea that the cops we have now aren't under their control, the way that teachers or other government workers are. They want to bring the police under the umbrella of "woke" politics. Seen from this perspective, the riots and looting of 2020 start to make a lot more sense.

# CHAPTER TWO

## The Collapse of New York City

I HAVE WALKED THE STREETS of Manhattan for many years, and it's been a long time since I felt threatened or menaced. Throughout the last decade, New York City has grown dirtier and less pleasant, but slowly. Now, like a frog being boiled in water, I and many others have suddenly noticed that the city is tinged with overt hostility. This isn't a fantasy, as many liberal critics sneer. The streets are noticeably populated with mentally ill, homeless, or drug-addicted individuals. And an opportunistic, criminal element has emerged to prey on our vulnerabilities.

A few months into the COVID pandemic in 2020, during which we were all supposed to be locked in our homes twiddling our thumbs, emerging only for quick, masked dashes for supplies, the George Floyd protests broke out. Tens of thousands of aggrieved demonstrators poured into the streets and parks, and the rest of us were told that their protests were okay because police violence is

also a "public health emergency," so we could keep our complaints
or questions to ourselves.

My wife and I were living with our baby on Ninth Avenue at
the time. Wildcat marches went on at any time of day or night,
sometimes two or three each day. Protestors smashed windows and
yelled at pedestrians. "Fire, fire, gentrifier! Black people used to live
here!" chanted gleeful agitators, threatening to burn down neighborhoods on the dubious grounds that the residents were occupying stolen land.

As I watched an impromptu midafternoon march head the
wrong way up a busy avenue, blocking traffic, I asked some police
officers what they thought of the situation. After all, you need a permit to march in the street. "Go ask the mayor," one cop said with a
shrug. "He says to leave them alone."

I saw video footage of protestors blocking traffic on 42nd
Street and Fifth Avenue. They moved menacingly on cars that
wouldn't turn around, in some cases puncturing tires and beating on the windows. When a frightened driver edged through the
scrum to get away, the protestors would howl in outrage, screaming that they were being run over. Their friends in public office
then took to social media, demanding that the police track down
and arrest the driver. The media showed video of the incident on
a repeating loop. The driver, Kathleen Casillo, was charged with
reckless endangerment. Offered a plea deal carrying a light sentence of community service, Casillo rejected the plea, asserting
that she was acting reasonably in racing to get away from a threatening mob. Her case is pending, and she could face seven years in
prison if found guilty.

Lawlessness pervaded the city, along with a gnawing suspicion
that the police and city government weren't invested in protecting
the citizenry. New York, along with many other cities in America,
appeared to be on a precipice.

## BACK TO THE FUTURE

In the eighties and early nineties, American cities were beset by a wave of homicide and violent crime associated with the emergence of crack cocaine. Crack, easy to prepare and convenient to sell in small "rocks," offered a quick, intense hit when smoked. Though crack is chemically the same substance as powdered cocaine, selling it in small, cheap doses made its use and spread prevalent in low-income urban areas by the mid-eighties. The control of local markets, sometimes as small as one or two city blocks, led to intense competition between rival gangs.

Between 1985 and 1993, the nation's murder rate rose dramatically, from about 8 per 100,000 to about 10 per 100,000: a 25 percent increase. Virtually all this increase was driven by murders of young black males by other young black males. The murder rate for black males aged 14 to 17 increased 250 percent, and the rate for their older brothers went up by approximately double. During the same period, the homicide rate for whites stayed more or less flat.

By 1993, according to the U.S. Department of Justice Bureau of Justice Statistics, black men under the age of 24, while amounting to only 1 percent of the population, committed 35 percent of all murders. The rise in murder and other violent crime during this period was caused by drugs. Gangs fought bloody wars over turf, and addicts committed crime in order to feed their addiction. At the peak of the crack epidemic, close to 75 percent of those murders were drug related.[1]

Communities across the nation were devastated by violence associated with the illegal drug trade. When you read histories of this period, or watch PBS documentaries or listen to celebrity politicians mouth off about it, you will mostly hear about the damage that was done by "overpolicing" our nation's cities. The anti-crime efforts that our police departments pursued so vigorously, we were being told, were just a racist war on black neighborhoods.

But the reality is that drugs and violence had already corroded our inner cities, not the intervention of law enforcement. New York City, where my father was a cop, was no exception. In fact, it was the prime example of how bad a city could get. New York is the place I know best, and it serves as a microcosm of the whole nation, demonstrating how good policy and bad policy can make or break a city's fortunes.

Immediately after World War II, New York City was bustling and prosperous. It had a broad working-class population and a strong industrial base. The city had more than one million manufacturing jobs in 1947. In 1950, more than 300,000 people worked in the city's garment industry alone. The city's waterfront in Manhattan and Brooklyn was a source of good union longshoreman jobs. New York City was relatively safe in those days. There was certainly crime, but murders occurred less than once a day on average across the whole city throughout the forties and fifties.

By the 1960s, the city's industrial base, which offered a step up into the unionized working and middle class for people with not much education and maybe a few years of skills training, began to shrink. Manufacturers began the process, which continues today, of looking for cheaper labor elsewhere. They relocated their factories to the South, and then abroad to Mexico or Central America, and later to Asia.

At the same time, shipping transitioned to containerization, so there was no need for longshoremen to load and unload loose cargo from holds. Waterfront jobs shifted to ports in New Jersey that could accommodate the movement of containers to trucks and rail traffic. New York City's busy waterfront, the center of city commerce for centuries, became derelict.

These economic phenomena thinned out the opportunity for

work for unskilled or low-skilled labor in New York. The white middle class began to move out of the cities, and their apartments were taken by black and Latino newcomers. This is sometimes called "white flight," the idea being that whites were terrified of living among nonwhites. White flight is typically described as irrational racism. But the massive demographic change that affected the composition of urban neighborhoods was, in many cases, accompanied by rising crime. Once-safe communities became dangerous, and many residents chose to look elsewhere. People didn't leave their neighborhoods out of irrational fears—things got measurably worse quickly.

Many children and grandchildren of immigrants who had attained some part of the American Dream moved out of the outer boroughs of New York City—primarily meaning Brooklyn, Queens, and the Bronx—and into suburban developments on Long Island, in New Jersey, or in Westchester County. This dynamic continued to thin out the city's tax base and led also to a hollowing out of real estate values. Neighborhoods like Brownsville and East New York in Brooklyn, or the Grand Concourse in the Bronx, which had been solidly working-class, became slums. Meanwhile, liberals in City Hall—following the lead of Washington, where Lyndon Johnson launched a "War on Poverty"—were expanding the social services safety net, offering cash assistance to the poor and needy.

## "ROOT CAUSES"

Whatever the good intentions of setting up New York City as a welfare state were, they backfired dramatically. Handing out welfare benefits created a "culture of dependency" among a new underclass mostly composed of African Americans and Puerto Ricans. Welfare payments were contingent on low household income. This encouraged young women to have babies outside of marriage because the government essentially took on the traditional role of the father. Rates of single motherhood soared among black women.

Some people on the Left promote the myth that the black family has always been matriarchally focused, perhaps owing to its roots in West African family structure. Others suggest that the legacy of slavery disrupted black patterns of family formation. But these are myths. The great economist Thomas Sowell has shown that black marriage rates were high through slavery, rose after the Civil War, and were comparable to if not higher than white marriage rates through the first half of the twentieth century. Having children out of wedlock was no more acceptable in the black community than it was among whites. The vast majority of black children before the 1960s grew up in two-parent households.[2,3]

Out-of-wedlock births in 1946 comprised 3 percent of all babies born. By 1959, that number had risen to 8 percent. In 2010, the rate was 45 percent city-wide, and in the Bronx, 70 percent of births were to single mothers. Today, three-quarters of all black children nationwide are born out of wedlock. The United States leads the world in single-parent households.[4]

When abortion was made legal in America, many people assumed that illegitimate births would decline. But the opposite happened, because the tradition of the "shotgun marriage" disappeared. It used to be that people were socially expected to get married if the woman got pregnant. But after the Supreme Court's ruling in *Roe v. Wade* in 1973, the sense that men bear equal responsibility for raising kids faded away. Now that *Roe* has been overturned, it's an open question as to how men and women will respond to the new environment in states that outlaw abortion.

I'm not trying to shame anyone. There are women who have kids without being married to their fathers. But women for whom this scenario works usually have resources, have children later in life, and the dads are involved in the kids' lives to some extent. It's one thing if you already have a college degree and a career, and can afford to hire nannies, and you have a baby at age forty. It's totally different if you are seventeen, dropped out of high school, the baby's father is out of the picture or unreliable, and you live with your mother or grandmother.

Creating incentives for women to have babies out of wedlock sent the African American community into a spiral of social dysfunction. Growing up without a father around, despite what some elite feminists insist, is terrible for children, especially boys. Generations of fatherless families have created men who lack proper role models, have not developed internal structures of discipline, and lack motivation to succeed in the normal channels of social life. There is research that strongly suggests that the increase in out-of-wedlock births causes increased crime rates twenty years later.[5] In any case, we don't need sociologists to explain that two-parent families provide better outcomes—both financially and personally—for kids.

By the middle to late 1960s, areas of New York City, especially the South Bronx, the Lower East Side, and parts of Brooklyn, had taken on extreme slum characteristics. Real estate values cratered. Rent rolls couldn't cover the cost of maintaining buildings, and landlords began to abandon buildings entirely, letting the city take over their properties, which weren't worth the cost of the back taxes owed on them.

The city would pay to relocate families who had been left homeless because of fire. This created an incentive to start fires in your own house. Landlords got in on the action, too, starting fires to collect on insurance policies. Arson created vast blocks of rubble, resembling Tokyo or Berlin after aerial bombing raids.

The Left always likes to say that crime can be traced to certain "root causes." Congresswoman Alexandria Ocasio-Cortez famously said that a massive rise in crime and shootings in New York City in 2020 was caused by "desperate people" who were "stealing bread to feed their families." But there is very little evidence that poverty causes crime. During the 1930s, hundreds of people were living in shanties in the middle of Central Park and thousands more were sleeping in the streets. There was massive unemployment and real hunger, but crime was relatively low. In 1940, for instance, there were only 275 murders. People were certainly "desperate," and there probably were actual cases of parents stealing bread for their children. But we didn't see a spike in violent crime. Similarly, the poverty rate in New York City went up between 1989 and 2016, from 18.8 percent to 19.5 percent. But the homicide rate dropped by about 90 percent over that same period.[6]

By 1969, there were more than one thousand murders in New York City, and the number began to climb steadily over the next twenty years. New York became a frightening city, and not only because murder was on the rise. All the major crimes went up: rape more than doubled, aggravated assault more than tripled, and robbery was five times as frequent. And that's just the crimes that were reported—as time went on, it became common for people not to bother calling the cops, because there was an assumption that they wouldn't do anything anyway.

New Yorkers experienced a degradation in their neighborhoods that severely impacted their quality of life. Subway trains were covered in graffiti as "artists" competed to outdo each other in covering whole cars with their street names, as rolling monuments to their own egos. Vandals would deface monuments and ordinary buildings, competing to overwrite each other's work. Stolen cars were stripped and left to rust along the side of city highways or set on fire on remote streets. City parks were dangerous and unpleasant. Prostitutes openly offered themselves outside the entrances to the Hudson River tunnel crossings. Drug dealing, gambling, and public intoxication were considered part of the backdrop of city life. Outside of elite neighborhoods, the city was dirty, and life could be harsh.

## POLICING

After World War II, policing in American cities became more professionalized. For the previous hundred years, being a policeman was a patronage position handed out as a reward for political services, often passed down within families or largely restricted to certain ethnic groups. The new way of policing was based on a civil service model, with tests and centralized hiring, instead of favoritism by local ward bosses. Part of the new theory of policing was to get cops off the beat patrol and into patrol cars. Officers would have responsibility for widespread areas that they knew less well. This system, it was thought, would cut down on corruption.

Isolating police in their cars, however, detached them from the neighborhoods they were supposed to protect and led to increased tensions between cops and the community. The role of the police became reactive: they would wait for a call from the radio dispatcher and then race to the scene of a crime, which was usually already over. "Crime prevention" was the job of social workers, whereas real cops dealt with serious crime and catching bad guys in the act. Local concerns, general disorder, or low-level misdemeanors were considered a waste of time.

Leftists in favor of defunding the police make this point all the time: Why are the police wasting precious resources arresting shoplifters or trespassers, when they should be out apprehending killers and rapists? But this gets policing and safe communities all wrong.

By the early 1980s it was clear that fighting serious crime wasn't stopping it. The crime associated with the crack epidemic led to spiraling violence that saw 2,245 murders in 1990, or more than six per day. That same year, dozens of "black car" drivers—livery drivers who mostly worked in the outer boroughs—were killed in their cars, usually for less than fifty dollars. Rather than risk getting murdered, more than 25 percent of the livery drivers quit.

New York City became increasingly scary. There's a reason movies like *Escape from New York* or *The Warriors*, which depicted Gotham as an insane hellhole of violence and savagery, were set where they were. In July 1983, Diana Ross held a concert in Central Park that ended in mob violence, with gangs attacking, robbing, and beating other attendees after the show ended. Dozens were injured and dozens arrested.

Shortly before Christmas in 1984, Bernhard Goetz, a white, nerdy-looking electrical engineer, got on the downtown 2 train. Four black teenagers—who, as they later testified, were on their way to Times Square to break into and rob arcade games—approached Goetz and demanded five dollars. Goetz, who had been mugged on the subway previously, pulled out an unlicensed revolver and shot all of them, wounding one of them badly. Goetz became a folk hero to many New Yorkers, who saw him as a model of a little guy who wouldn't stand for being a victim. Others saw him as a racist vigilante who went looking for an excuse to shoot black kids. In any case, a jury found him not guilty of serious assault charges, convicting him only on a weapons violation.

The Central Park jogger case of April 1989 saw dozens of teenagers rampaging through the park beating up cyclists and pedestrians, with one of them accused of raping and maiming a jogger and leaving her for dead. The following year, a family of tourists from Utah got on the subway in Manhattan, planning to take a short trip uptown to have dinner. They were attacked by a gang of teenagers, who mugged and beat the parents and then stabbed their twenty-two-year-old son, Brian Watkins, to death.

These crimes horrified the nation. The Watkins case prompted full-page headlines demanding action. Rising crime stained the record of New York City's first black mayor, David Dinkins, who is somewhat unfairly associated with the "bad old days," when the city hit rock bottom. Dinkins was an imperfect mayor. I would say that his handling of the Crown Heights riots—when angry black New Yorkers waged a pogrom against their Jewish neighbors after a little boy from their community was killed in a traffic accident—was flawed, and more aggressive police action, taken much earlier, could have prevented the mob violence that wound up killing a Jewish rabbinical student. A commission appointed by then-governor Mario Cuomo, in fact, found that my father—who was First Deputy Commissioner at the time—had been excluded from an operational role, and that, "given the seriousness of the disturbances, it is unfortunate that the First Deputy did not assume a role in coordinating the development and implementation of a different strategy sooner." Ultimately, his talents were employed and my father led the efforts to quell the riot.

But the received narrative about crime in New York—that Dinkins was a failure, and the city was saved by his successor—demands some major revision. First of all, many of the uglier crimes that are associated with New York City's bad years occurred during Ed Koch's third term. The Central Park jogger case, for example, took place under Koch, as did the Robert Chambers "preppie murder" case, the racially motivated Howard Beach incident, and the murder of Yusuf Hawkins. The crack cocaine epidemic hit cities across the country, and no police department was fully prepared to deal with the chaos it spawned.

## COMEBACK

It's true that crime peaked in the Dinkins years, but it's also true that it began to decline then, too. Many of the changes that led to New York's renaissance were implemented under Mayor Dinkins. My father, Raymond Kelly, was appointed NYPD commissioner by Dinkins in October 1992 and served in that role for the remainder of Dinkins's only term. As First Deputy Commissioner under Commissioner Lee Brown, and then as commissioner, my father authored and set in motion a series of reforms and a change in general orientation that revolutionized policing in New York City and set the stage for its rebirth as the safest big city in the nation.

In 1982, criminologists George Kelling and James Q. Wilson published an essay in the *Atlantic* magazine called "Broken Windows: The Police and Neighborhood Safety." They argued that the radio-car strategy of policing didn't work, because it was based on reacting to crime. "Patrol cars arrive," they explained, "an occasional arrest occurs but crime continues and disorder is not abated."[7]

Kelling later pointed out that "fear of crime is one of the worst consequences of crime." Even in a high-crime area, most people will not be victims of crime on an average day. But they are afraid to go outside at night, double-lock their doors, don't let their kids play outside, and leave their jewelry at home. Fear dominates people's lives and colors their experience.

"For every person mugged in the park there are hundreds or thousands who do not walk in the park," Kelling noted. But he went further, pointing out that even evidence of disorder—kids hanging out and blocking the sidewalk; beggars; open prostitution and gambling; drug sales and drug use—is just as important as "real" crime in creating a climate of fear among law-abiding people who want to live normally and be able to enjoy public space securely. Graffiti or public urination may not call for the death penalty, but their presence sends a signal that authority has broken down. Nobody wants to raise their kids in an "anything goes" atmosphere.

Kelling and Wilson put forth the "broken windows" theory of crime. According to them, disorder leads inevitably to more disorder, and then to crime. They wrote, famously, "If a window in a building is broken and is left unrepaired, all the rest of the windows will soon be broken." It's a little like having a bunch of roommates who are careless about housework. If one guy leaves a plate in the sink, then everyone will become sloppy about doing the dishes.

Soon the whole place is a pigsty, because nobody is taking responsibility for the common good.

Daniel Patrick Moynihan, a U.S. senator from New York who was also an ambassador and a sociologist, called this dynamic "defining deviancy down." You gradually lower the bar of acceptability until what seemed intolerable last year is the new normal. Like how in New York City just a few years ago it was considered inappropriate to smoke marijuana in public, but now it is practically normal to see people smoking it on the subway.

The way to fight crime, then, isn't so much to speed after criminals after you get the call from the dispatcher, as it is to promote orderliness at the neighborhood level. This is the essence of community policing, which my father promoted strongly at One Police Plaza at the beginning of Mayor Dinkins's term in 1990. Establishing public order doesn't start with preventing murder; it begins at the street level, with preventing vandalism, littering, and low-level quality-of-life disorder.

## BROKEN THEORY

The broken windows theory is misrepresented by Defunders as some kind of medieval system of swift, severe punishment—like the Zulu king Shaka, who imposed the death penalty for a first offense, and thereby achieved rigid compliance with his rule. But the idea of the broken windows theory and community policing is that orderly neighborhoods are self-sustaining. It's easier and more productive for a household of roommates to keep things clean on a daily basis than to live in a dump most of the time and then have to clean everything all at once.

Defunders and radical leftists often point out that low-crime, usually well-off communities don't have a lot of police officers everywhere enforcing the law. They say that this is proof that police aren't the key to public safety—what poor, high-crime neighborhoods need is "resources." But they are confusing cause and effect. Low-crime, stable communities are self-sustaining because disorderly behavior—public drug sales, gambling, littering—isn't tolerated. High-crime neighborhoods require help from the police to get the virtuous circle of orderliness started.

One of Kelly's biggest initiatives was the "Safe Streets, Safe City" approach, which became the signature public safety program of the Dinkins administration. Taking a community policing approach, Safe Streets, Safe City set forth a "battle plan against fear." When Mayor Dinkins took over, the NYPD only had about 24,000 uniformed officers; he proposed to add 8,000 more. The program would cost close to $2 billion over four years, and would expand the capacity of Rikers Island, the city's jail, by 3,000 beds; "civilianize" administrative functions so uniformed cops could hit the streets; and assign a transit officer to every subway train overnight.

It's amazing to think that David Dinkins—considered one of New York's most liberal mayors—wanted to expand Rikers Island, which today's officials want to close.

Rather than focusing on major crimes, which are hard to predict and prevent, the NYPD under Lee Brown and my father made a strategic choice to prevent lower-level disorder. "We start with the premise of the broken windows theory—it is important to maintain a sense of order, and for people to feel the public spaces are available to them," explained Jeremy Travis, deputy commissioner of police for legal matters under Lee Brown and Ray Kelly. "Our belief is that if you take care of the little things, the big things will follow."

One of the major demonstrations of the power of broken windows policing was aimed at the city's notorious "squeegee men." These guys would stand outside tunnel entrances or at red lights and approach stopped cars, holding a spray bottle and a squeegee or just a rag, and start "cleaning" your windshield, typically without asking. Then they would demand a tip, which they didn't consider optional. Many drivers had their windshield wipers or car antennas—remember those?—torn off, or would get spit on if they didn't hand over some change or a few bucks.

Everyone loathed the squeegee men. Unlike most beggars or panhandlers, they were obnoxious and often threatening. There was nothing remotely charming about having some filthy bum lurch toward your car and start aggressively smearing a dirty squeegee across your windshield. Tourists today may marvel at the subway "showtime" dancers whom I and most New Yorkers find annoying, but nobody found any entertainment value in the squeegee guys.

As NYPD commissioner under Dinkins, my father cracked down on the squeegee men and got them off the streets. This was a huge victory for New York City. Motorists, including tourists or families in from the suburbs for a night out, were relieved that they did not have to deal with this incredible, unnecessary nuisance. Many people wondered why it took so long to clean up this mess—and if they could do that, what else was possible?

Dinkins ran for a second term, and the *New York Times* endorsed him, citing his appointment of my father as NYPD commissioner as an "important decision" that demonstrated Dinkins's competence. Rudy Giuliani won the 1993 election for mayor, largely on a law-and-order platform. Though murders went down in Dinkins's last year in office, they were still unacceptably high. Mayor Rudy appointed Bill Bratton as his police commissioner. Bratton had run the Transit Police when my father was First Deputy Commissioner of the NYPD, back when they were separate departments. Giuliani and Bratton get a lot of credit for bringing down crime in New York City. But there's a certain narrative that's been promoted rather vociferously in certain quarters that I think deserves review.

The narrative goes that the broken windows era of community

policing began with Giuliani and Bratton. All the credit for New York's turnaround goes to them. I don't want to cast aspersions on anyone or accuse them of lying. Suffice to say that every new mayor likes to make a clean sweep and take credit for anything good that happens.

But even Bratton acknowledges that major changes had already happened when he took over at 1PP. In his 1998 book, *Turnaround*, written before either he or my father had returned to the top spot at the NYPD, Bratton explained:

> This turnaround was effected by Dinkins and Kelly. When I arrived, we kept up the police presence and pressure. Ironically, Giuliani and I got the credit for their initiative, but understandably Giuliani was happy to take credit. . . . Only politics prevented David Dinkins and Ray Kelly from receiving their due.

Giuliani did so much for New York City. His press-pleasing lieutenant Bratton only stayed on the job for a little over two years. The heart and soul of policing was directed from City Hall. Those were solid years: in 1996, New York City recorded fewer than a thousand murders for the first time since 1968. Howard Safir, who replaced Bratton, was a former federal agent with deep experience fighting drug crime; he made bold moves to take back neighborhoods in Upper Manhattan and the Bronx from the gangs who had turned whole blocks into open-air drug marts, attracting buyers from Virginia to Boston. Bernard Kerik came in after Safir departed in 2000, rounding out the Giuliani years. Those eight years, during which murder dropped by almost 60 percent, were definitely significant in the history of New York. But it's important to acknowledge that David Dinkins and Ray Kelly were instrumental in setting the stage for that success.

My father returned to One Police Plaza in 2002 as NYPD commissioner under Mayor Michael Bloomberg, becoming the first commissioner to take on the role for a second nonconsecutive stint. He served for all twelve years of Bloomberg's three terms, and is the longest-serving commissioner in NYPD history.

Personalities and reputations aside, the important thing about the Dinkins-Giuliani-Bloomberg era is that there was consistent dedication to the principle of public safety. Thousands of lives were saved during that period—mostly black lives, I may add—and many billions of dollars of wealth were created as New York City prospered. The decline of the city in the eighties was reversed. Companies flocked to Manhattan and brought well-paid office workers with them.

Affluent people saw that they could walk the streets without fears of being mugged, and invested in luxury real estate that generated huge tax revenues. This increased revenue enabled the city to expand spending on social services and amenities that benefited everyone. And normal New Yorkers—millions of people who work for a living—were able to prosper, too. The schools improved, slowly. The trains were safe. Parents could let their kids play outside, and the parks were seeded with thick grass so people could play softball or soccer, or relax and look at the clouds while they picnicked with their families. New York became livable again.

Enforcement of quality-of-life violations was key to this turnaround. This didn't have to be zero-tolerance fascism, as the Defunders claim. There was no reason for cops to arrest every litterer or public drinker, but if they had an outstanding warrant or refused to show ID, then it was worthwhile bringing them to the station instead of giving them a ticket, or a desk appearance ticket (DAT). A DAT was essentially a notice to appear before a judge, but in the old days, scofflaws could just throw them away.

Similarly, people who jump the turnstile into the subway system in order to avoid paying their $2.75 fare may not be serious criminals. But a high proportion of serious criminals will try to beat the subway fare. Why not? If your whole perspective on life is opportunistic, and you habitually try to skirt or violate the law, or take advantage of security flaws in order to steal things, then paying a few bucks for a subway ride is a sucker's game. Defunders insist that arresting people for fare evasion is "criminalizing poverty," but if that's true, why do most poor people pay their fare? Liberals like to blame society for every criminal's bad life choices, but that detracts from the fact that most people of every income level respect the rules.

Broken windows policing doesn't mean that every infraction results in an arrest. But if someone jumps the turnstile repeatedly, then maybe a warning or a DAT isn't cutting it. Moreover, stopping people committing "minor" violations is a useful pretext for searching them for weapons. Cops frequently seized illegal guns from turnstile jumpers, making the subways safer, encouraging more people to ride without fear.

The question of stopping and searching people on the street has become enormously controversial, and even played a part in the 2020 presidential election, on the Democrat side. People have said that the practice as it was carried out in New York is essentially racist, and that Bloomberg and Kelly were the architects of a policy that unfairly and illegally swept up hundreds of thousands of innocent people into the jaws of the criminal justice system, condemning them to a life of stigma and social exclusion, if not a full-on life of crime.

"Stop, Question, and Frisk" (SQF) is an established police practice, and was found to be constitutional by the Supreme Court in 1968 in *Terry v. Ohio*. This case established that the police, if they have reasonable suspicion that someone is involved in criminal activity, can stop them for brief questioning. As part of this questioning, they are allowed to pat the suspect down outside their clothing to see if they are carrying a concealed weapon. Cops have used Terry stops or SQFs as an important tool. Can it be misused? Of course it can. Just like any tool can be misused. But just because you can use a hammer to smash car windows, that doesn't mean carpenters can't use it to drive nails.

## BLOOMBERG YEARS

When Mayor Bloomberg came to office in January 2002, murders and street crime were lower than they had been ten years before, but the new mayor and his police commissioner, Ray Kelly, knew that the city could do even better. Why be satisfied with 650 murders annually? Every murdered person represents an irreparable tear in the fabric of the city. How about working overtime to get as many illegal guns off the street as possible, in order to save more lives?

Bloomberg and Kelly implemented Operation Impact, which was a targeted effort to fight violent crime specifically where it was taking place. As it happened, these hot spots were primarily in black and Latino neighborhoods. Violent crime in New York City is a heavily segregated phenomenon: around 98 percent of shootings are committed by black or Latino people in any given year. If you are planning to fight crime in a serious way and take guns off the street, it follows that you have to go where the action is.

When my father ran the NYPD under David Dinkins, he was widely respected for his outreach to the black community. He went to black churches and other groups and talked to them frankly about Safe Streets, Safe City. He purposefully set about recruiting more nonwhite officers to make the NYPD reflect the demographics of the city. Kelly postponed a scheduled police examination in order to initiate a special minority recruitment drive. As a result, more qualified black and Latino candidates wound up on the passing list than ever before.

In the nineties, the NYPD's relations with minority communities suffered. A series of high-profile incidents tainted the NYPD and helped perpetuate the myth that the police are the enemy of New York City's black population.

The 1997 Abner Louima case, for example, was an utter scandal. Four white cops arrested Louima, who turned out to be totally innocent, for involvement in a minor street altercation. Louima was beaten up and raped with a broom handle. Louima's chief victimizer is still in prison for his crimes. In 1999, cops stopped Amadou Diallo on the street. As he reached to get his wallet, he was shot nineteen times and killed.

The following year, two undercover police officers approached Patrick Dorismond and said they wanted to buy marijuana. Dorismond dismissed them, saying he wasn't a drug dealer. A scuffle occurred, and Dorismond was shot and killed. There's no question that a great deal of bad will created these incidents between the NYPD and the black community.

When Ray Kelly returned to One Police Plaza, he wanted to repair relations with black New Yorkers. He had maintained his contacts with community leaders. Bloomberg and Kelly were committed to driving down crime. But they knew that an effective crime-fighting strategy would require buy-in from the black community. My father spoke to black leaders about how he would use street stops of people engaged in suspicious behavior in order to get illegal guns out of the hands of would-be killers. He assured them the practice would be judicious. His plan was met with overwhelming approval.

It's curious, looking back now, to note that the liberal media in New York City was skeptical that the Bloomberg-Kelly team would be able to preserve the gains that Giuliani had made in fighting crime. Giuliani, "America's Mayor" following the 9/11 attacks, had emerged as a hero, and it was impossible for local political reporters to conceive of anyone filling his shoes.

The practice of stop-and-frisk did increase under Bloomberg and Kelly, but so did its effectiveness and the accuracy of recording it. While a disproportionate number of black and Latino New Yorkers were stopped relative to their overall population, they were underrepresented relative to the rate of crime in their neighborhoods. Remember: 98 percent of shootings were and are perpetrated by black and Latino New Yorkers. When NYPD brass are deciding where to commit resources, they don't say, "Let's send the cops out to the black neighborhood." They look at the 911 calls and say, "Here's the blocks that need the most attention."

Defunders and other anti-cop activists tried to work up a scandal in regard to SQF, saying that it was like a military force invading minority neighborhoods and brutalizing the local youth. This became a theme in leftist coverage. The *Guardian* interviewed a guy named Keeshan who said he was "stopped and frisked more than 100 times," and was never arrested.[8] Jumaane Williams, the public advocate of New York—a city-wide elected position that has few substantive responsibilities except to provide the office-holder a platform to run for higher office (former mayor Bill de Blasio and current New York State attorney general Letitia James were public advocates)—has worked tirelessly to fight the practice. "Sixty-six percent of the stops are for people they believe to have weapons, 93 percent of the time there are no weapons found," Williams says.

That's true, as far as it goes, but if cops find a gun 7 percent of the time, and they were performing 500,000 stops annually, that's 35,000 illegal weapons taken off the streets. And that doesn't even account for the number of guns that criminals left at home because they didn't want to run the risk of getting stopped. As my father explained, half a million stops per year just means 10,000 patrol cops performing one stop-and-frisk weekly.

A loaded gun is an unwieldy hunk of metal weighing between a pound and a half and two pounds. It makes a distinctive bulge when carried in a jacket pocket or thrust into the back of a pair of pants. The average street criminal does not wear a properly sized and fitted holster. Rather, he shoves his gun wherever he can in his clothes and hopes it won't fall out. Cops know how to notice someone who keeps adjusting his pants, or who walks unnaturally trying to compensate for the awkward weight and shape of a concealed pistol.

As for the myth that the practice of stop-and-frisk brutalized and dehumanized black and Latino youth, scarring them irreparably and imposing the stigma of surveillance and criminality on them, let me ask a simple question: Where is all the video? YouTube and WorldStarHipHop both launched in 2005. The iPhone came out in 2007. "Viral videos" of all manner of street carnage and abusive police behavior have circulated for years. You can find tons of videos of leftist activists complaining about SQF. But there aren't many—if any—videos depicting the kind of brutality in relation to SQF that advocates insist was a hallmark and feature of the practice.

That's because Stop, Question, and Frisk was a humane, civilized policing practice that succeeded in driving down crime to unimaginably low levels. The year before Bloomberg took office and installed Ray Kelly as commissioner, New York recorded 649 murders—remarkable progress since the high ten years before of 2,245 homicides. But by the time Bloomberg left office twelve years later, he and my father had driven the number down by another half, to 335 killings. The last time the city had marked fewer than one murder per day had been 1958. And it was in large measure thanks to SQF, an important though not singular tool in the NYPD's tool kit.[9]

## WORST MAYOR EVER

When Bloomberg left office on the last day of 2013 after twelve years, he was replaced by Bill de Blasio, who managed to unravel decades of carefully engineered and maintained quality of life and public safety. It's hard to imagine now, after a decade of relentless cop bashing, but throughout the Bloomberg-Kelly years, the NYPD's poll numbers showed that the people of New York City had an increasingly positive view of the police. In 2013, 70 percent of New Yorkers had a positive approval of the NYPD, versus only 23 percent who disapproved. Ray Kelly had a 75 percent approval rating when he left his post.

A federal lawsuit over SQF was tied up in the courts—Shira Scheindlin, the judge who had ruled it to be unconstitutional, had been removed from the case because of her bias. Scheindlin had made her opposition to SQF clear in newspaper interviews, and then used improper influence to have the case assigned to her court. The circuit court made the unprecedented decision to put the case on hold and replace Judge Scheindlin because she had run afoul of the judicial Code of Conduct. This rebuke was an enormous slap in the face. One of de Blasio's first actions was to give up the city's appeal, which certainly would have succeeded. This is a case where the city was winning its appeal, yet for political reasons de Blasio dropped the case. In so doing, he agreed to place the NYPD under a federal monitor to keep its patrol policies under scrutiny.

Admitting, against all reason, that the NYPD's use of SQF was unconstitutional set the stage for the Defund movement to begin its long march to destroy policing. Over the next eight years of de

Blasio's term, he decriminalized such "minor" crimes as public urination, littering, and public intoxication. He signed legislation that
forced the police to inform suspects that they don't have to consent
to being searched. He appointed dozens of judges from the criminal justice reform community. He supported bail reform legislation
that has permitted serious criminals to walk free after committing
heinous crimes.

He encouraged the police to stop enforcing the law against
fare evasion and marijuana possession. Possibly the most absurd,
shameful moment in the history of law enforcement came when
he stood with his first NYPD commissioner, Bill Bratton, who
held up a large bag of oregano resembling marijuana, for the
cameras. "Persons found to be in possession of this amount of
marijuana, twenty-five grams or less, may be eligible to receive
a summons" instead of being arrested, Bratton announced in
November 2014. While he promised that "burning" marijuana
would remain arrestable, the image of the city's top cop smiling
while holding out what seemed like a big bag of pot sent out the
message that New York was embracing its decriminalization and
subsequent normalization.

Pot is now legal in New York and the effects are dire. People
sell it, illegally, on card tables in full view of police in the city's
parks. Technically kids aren't supposed to be able to get it, but the
restrictions are laughable. You smell it literally everywhere, and it's
disgusting. Walk past any construction site, and you catch a whiff.
Decades of pro-pot propaganda have miseducated the public that
marijuana is harmless, and that concern about its use is something
to snicker at. But marijuana is not a safe drug. Technicians have
refined it through hybridization to a frightening level of potency.
People who are mentally ill or who have a tendency toward mental
illness can be triggered by pot and enter schizophrenic states. In
the sixties and seventies, hip stoners laughed at squares warning

about "reefer madness," but it is clearly connected to psychotic epi-sodes and violence.[10] The marijuana establishment pretends that it can treat all manner of ailments, but in fact the Food and Drug Administration has not approved the drug as a treatment for any disease.[11]

Under Bill de Blasio, and now into the administration of his successor, Eric Adams, New York City has gravely deteriorated. Twenty years of solid policing practice have been methodically dismantled. When Adams was elected to office, many moderates breathed a sigh of relief that the more radical Defunder candidates had lost. "Adams will turn the crime problem around," I heard from many people, including conservatives who were heartened that we had put a former cop into City Hall.

But while Adams rose through the ranks of the NYPD to become a captain, he was never really a cop in the eyes of many of his colleagues. He recounts that he wanted to join the NYPD after getting beaten up in a precinct house as a teenager, in order to "change" things from within, but it was probably so he could get his revenge on what he saw as the white power structure in charge. Adams's entire career in the NYPD was built around attacking the department, first as president of the "Grand Coun-cil of Guardians," and then as the founder of "100 Blacks in Law Enforcement Who Care." He was part of the lawsuit to end stop-and-frisk. He palled around with race-baiters like Louis Farra-khan and Al Sharpton, and moonlighted as Sharpton's bodyguard, saying that he wanted to prevent his assassination by a "racist sys-tem" inside the NYPD. He has accused "white men in suits" of being the ones who bring guns into black communities, thereby causing the "ongoing genocidal murder in urban America."[12]

Nothing in Eric Adams's professional life suggests that he is remotely qualified for the job he has. For starters, he was evidently living in another state, New Jersey, when he was running for mayor of New York City. There are thousands of police officers serving today who know more about law enforcement than he does. He arguably lacks the management, administrative, and even political skills to run a city as complex as New York. He has used outright racist language in public, calling members of the NYPD "crackers" and complaining that reporters who weren't black couldn't accurately tell his story. He is enamored with the nightlife and his newfound celebrity. To me, he seems more interested in the perks of the job than actually doing the job. And, so far, he's getting away with it.

Even if Adams really wanted to crack down on crime and disorder—which, based on his record, I strongly doubt—he would have a tough time doing it. The problem is that progressives at the city and state level have dismantled the machinery of public safety in New York. Working legislatively, judicially, and through the offices of prosecutors, they have sabotaged the city. Stop-and-frisk is largely off the table. Local prosecutors won't even bring illegal gun possession charges unless the perp has also committed some grave felony. The state has made it impossible to hold serious violent criminals in jail even for a night or two to force them to "cool off."

A suspect who chooses not to be arrested and fights back can't be brought to the ground using any traditional means. Any pressure applied to the back or diaphragm is now illegal and can subject the arresting officer to criminal charges. The state has also removed the qualified immunity that most public servants enjoy, which gives them the presumption of operating in good faith in their interactions with the public. Now, New York City cops who search a suspect or use force can be held personally liable if a jury finds that they acted unreasonably, even if their actions were in line with existing precedent. Eric Adams restored the anti-crime unit that de Blasio had eliminated, but put them in uniform, an action that defeats the purpose of a dedicated undercover anti-crime squad.

The point of these laws—and others—is to make cops second-guess their actions. The Defunders would like to cut police budgets, but having failed to do so, they have worked another angle, which is to make effective policing impossible.

It took a few years for everything to fall into place, but by the end of de Blasio's second term, the city had begun to fall apart. The murder rate in 2020 spiked by over 40 percent—that was unprecedented in recorded history. Yes, as the progressives love to tell us, it's still lower than it used to be—but so what? Lots of things aren't "as bad" as they used to be—like infant mortality, for instance. But if infant mortality suddenly rose by 40 percent, I assure you people would be upset, even if the rate was still low compared to 150 years ago.

The first half of 2022 saw four homicides on the subway. It used to be that an average year would see one, or at most two. There were years that went by when zero women in New York City were murdered by strangers. Now it happens frequently. Robbery under Adams is up 40 percent city-wide year to date, and felony assault is up almost 20 percent. Shoplifting has been effectively decriminalized, and thieves routinely walk out of stores with whatever they want, knowing that the store clerks are generally told not to try to stop them, and that even if the police do arrest them, they will be set free almost immediately. Pharmacies across the city are shutting down rather than take mounting losses from crooks who mosey out with bags of expensive goods. High-end retailers on Madison Avenue now keep their doors locked and buzz clients in, or simply stay closed and ask their regular customers to make appointments.

New York City is on a downward spiral. Jose Alba, a sixty-one-year-old grocery store worker, was attacked by a thug who was angry that Alba wouldn't let his girlfriend have a bag of chips without paying. While being beaten up, Alba managed to grab a knife and stab his attacker, who died. Alba, whom many New Yorkers applauded as a hero, was charged with murder. The charges were eventually dropped, but this case summed up the official attitude toward crime: just lie back and let it happen. Gangs of muggers targeting lone joggers or pedestrians have reemerged in Manhattan, and a new generation of New Yorkers is learning not to take safety for granted anymore.[13]

It is no longer unusual to walk around good neighborhoods and see drug addicts lurching around like zombies or defecating on the sidewalk. The city, to its credit, will clear tent encampments if they get too big, but they quickly get set up elsewhere. We have experience in living memory of how bad things can get, and retain the knowledge of how to avoid it or turn things around. But it's not clear any longer that we have the will to do what's necessary.

# CHAPTER THREE

## The New Religion of Antiracism

THE MOVEMENT AGAINST THE POLICE, borders, orderly neighborhoods, and law in general is all based in a set of myths that have been relentlessly shoved into the American consciousness and have not received sufficient pushback from sensible people—though some have tried. These myths have divided the country and set us at one another's throats. Or, really, they've set half the country at the throats of the other half, who are baffled and trying to figure out how to deal.

Part of the problem is that Americans are typically careful about causing offense. You know the old rule about how religion and politics are not fit topics for dinner table conversation? That's because, in a diverse society, it's better just to live and let live.

Now, that's a fine way to run a polite society. But it ceases to work if one part of the country decides that everything the other part does is offensive. They will apologize and try to "do better" for a while, but eventually people start to feel backed into a corner if you call them out all the time, for everything.

That's what's happened in America. A bizarre ideology that goes by many names—"critical race theory"; "white fragility"; "systemic racism"; "diversity, equity, and inclusion"; "wokeness"—has spewed out of academia, the elite media, and the offices of richly endowed nonprofit organizations, and the runoff has found its way into the crevices and corners of every institution in America. Libraries, the Boy Scouts, elementary schools, churches, workplaces—there is no hiding from this pernicious dogma that has reached down the gullet of American life, grabbed hold of the guts, and turned the whole country inside out.

What are the principles of this wicked creed? Foremost, that America is built on a lie. Though the Founders of the nation talked a good game about the God-given equality of all people, it was all a screen for them to entrench their own power as white, property-owning men. The whole point of America was to create a country ruled by whites, who would wield the whip hand over everyone else.

The standard narrative of American history—that slavery was a grievous iniquity, but one that the country has steadily overcome—is inverted. Life, they contend, is not measurably better for black people today than it was fifty, or even 150, years ago. Movie and television star Whoopi Goldberg made this point in 2022 when she told Chuck Schumer, the Senate majority leader:

> You vowed to call a vote on major voting rights legislation in time for Martin Luther King Day next week. I just want—I want to ask you this because it's irritating me to the nth degree. Why are we still talking about my right as an American to vote?
>
> I still feel like suddenly black people . . . are where we were under the Emancipation Proclamation. What is happening? Why are we still fighting this this way? What's . . . going to change?

The Emancipation Proclamation, issued in 1863 during the Civil War, freed the slaves in all areas under Union control. Mega-celebrity Whoopi Goldberg, who has been in the public eye consistently for about forty years, said that the plight of black people in the United States—where she has the rare distinction of having won an Academy Award, a Grammy, an Emmy, and a Tony—is the same now as it was under the Confederacy.

One would think that Senator Schumer—a graduate of Harvard Law School—might have corrected Goldberg, or at least qualified her comment. After all, America elected and reelected a black man to be president, and a black woman to be vice president. But no—he agreed with her, saying that she was "one hundred percent right." In fact, Schumer explained, things are headed downhill for African Americans. "It's not just staying the same," he warned. "It's going to get worse if we don't do something."

This exchange, aired on *The View* and heard by millions, is nothing unusual. It has become the standard perspective for millions of Americans and is taught in schools as a revisionist history that is, in the minds of its proponents, setting the record straight. Bestselling books over the last decade have advanced this thesis, and while their arguments are empty and tissue-thin, the media and academia have given their authors a platform and a megaphone through which they have been able to present their bizarro version of America.

## SLAVERY NEVER ENDED

*The New Jim Crow*, by law professor Michelle Alexander, came out in 2010 and became a bestseller in 2012, right around the time that Trayvon Martin was killed. It was at this time, you may recall, that Barack Obama decided to stop being our first postracial president, and instead imagine himself to the people of America as Trayvon's dad. "My main message is to the parents of

Trayvon Martin. You know, if I had a son, he'd look like Trayvon," Obama said. "All of us as Americans are going to take this with the seriousness it deserves. . . . All of us have to do some soul searching to figure out how something like this has happened."

(This expression, "looks like," really sets my teeth on edge. You hear this all the time. "I want a president who looks like me." Or, "Kids need teachers who look like them." So is it supposed to be acceptable by these terms to say that black people look alike, or Asians all look the same? "What are you complaining about? That politician over there looks like you!" People are individuals—the country I grew up in was one where we accepted that.)

The thesis of *The New Jim Crow*, which really set the tone of race relations for the next decade and more, is that the system of white supremacy in the South—the legal racial discrimination that defined relations between blacks and whites from the late nineteenth century through the passage of civil rights legislation in the mid-sixties—never really ended. What happened instead is that America submerged its racial oppression in the guise of public safety. "Human rights champion Bryan Stevenson," Alexander explains, "has observed that 'slavery didn't end; it evolved.'"

According to Alexander, prisons, jails, parole and probation officers, school safety agents, and certainly police officers and prosecutors form the outlines of the American system of mass incarceration. This system of control is as vast and unaccountable as the Soviet gulag system that Aleksandr Solzhenitsyn described, but in key ways it is even worse—because it is based around race. "We have not ended racial caste in America; we have merely redesigned it," she informs us.

The idea that our whole society is ordered as a white supremacist surveillance state, designed from top to bottom to oppress black people in order to enrich whites, received a fuller hearing from *New York Times* writer Nikole Hannah-Jones, whose "1619 Project" was a major effort to resituate the origin story of the United States from 1776—when the colonists declared independence from Britain—to 1619, the year that slaves were first transported to North America. The project sought to explain how "anti-black racism runs in the very DNA of this country," which was explicitly founded, Hannah-Jones absurdly insists, in order to preserve the "slavocracy" in the face of the imminent abolition of slavery by the British.

To say that the American Revolution was really a counter-revolution for the continuation of slavery is history squeezed through a sieve. Not only did the 1619 Project offer no evidence from the copious writings of the Founding Fathers to support this bold contention, but Hannah-Jones is saying that all the liberty-loving people around the world who have been inspired by the American Revolution and the words of the Declaration of Independence are fools and dupes. Frederick Douglass, who was born a slave, praised the signers of the Declaration as "brave men" and hailed "the great principles of political freedom and of natural justice, embodied in that Declaration of Independence."

The 1619 Project is riddled with errors, which have been rigorously and scrupulously identified by scholars and researchers from all political perspectives. The idea that the Revolution was carried out so slaveowners could keep their slaves has no basis in reality. In fact, the broad assumption in the 1770s was that slavery would soon die out. Men like our second president, John Adams, were staunchly antislavery. Matthew Desmond, a Princeton sociologist, claims that double-entry accounting, which all historians know had its roots in medieval Italy, was invented by an obscure southern plantation manager in the 1830s. This proves, according to Desmond, that modern capitalism's "roots twist back to slave-labor camps." This kind of twisted logic characterizes all of woke history: bad things that happened three hundred years ago matter more now than ever, while positive things happening all around us don't mean anything.

This historical illiteracy didn't stop Hannah-Jones from winning a Pulitzer Prize, writing a bestselling book, and receiving other accolades. But the real measure of the success of the 1619 Project—and possibly the reason for its inception to begin with—was how readily it was adopted for use in the classroom. "A re-education is necessary," explains the Project, which details the supposed "educational malpractice" that takes place in America, where schoolchildren don't learn about slavery, or at best "graduate with a poor understanding of how slavery shaped our country."

Now, I don't know about you, but when I went to elementary school in the 1970s and high school in the 1980s, we certainly learned about slavery. And it wasn't sugarcoated. I have talked to a lot of people, including people my parents' age, and they all say the same thing. I would say that there are very few people alive today who went to school in America who didn't learn that slavery was a bestial and horrific practice that ended because hundreds of thousands of mostly white men died on the battlefields of the Civil War.

The left-wing Pulitzer Center has worked hard to get the curricular version of the 1619 Project into the hands of teachers in 4,500 classrooms. The goal is clear: to indoctrinate children in a warped, pernicious understanding of America as fundamentally evil. Funding for this specific project has come from Meta (formerly Facebook Inc.) and the Open Society Foundations. The Open Society, founded and funded by billionaire financier George Soros, who also funded Black Lives Matter, the "Women's March," and other groups that formed the core of the "Resistance" to Trump. The 1619 Project must be understood in this context.

## ANTIRACISM VS. NONRACISM

In the weeks after George Floyd died outside a Minneapolis corner store where he was passing counterfeit money while high on massive amounts of drugs, America was rocked by riots and protests that went on interminably. In New York City, where I live, we were subjected to nonstop marches and blockades of traffic, which no one was allowed to cross or question. Radicals strutted around with megaphones screaming "White silence is violence!" and similar mottos. Thousands of cops were attacked and injured, stores were looted, and dozens of vehicles were torched and destroyed.

Around this time, the idea of "antiracism" started to come up frequently, especially in connection to a book called *How to Be an Antiracist*, by Ibram X. Kendi. Now, I consider myself against racism, and a nonracist. As I said earlier, I grew up in a house where my dad had black colleagues and friends who came over for parties and barbecues all the time. He had black bosses whom he respected.

Later, I was in the Marines. I had black officers above me and black Marines below me and black fellow pilots. We spent time together in training and in missions and on board ships for months at a time. I've had black colleagues and friends my entire adult life. It would never occur to me to prejudge anyone based on their color. Black people are, first and foremost, individuals, and I was raised to treat every individual equally, on his or her merits.

But that's not what is meant by being an "antiracist," in Kendi's sense of the word. In fact, according to Kendi, a bestselling author and director of the Center for Antiracist Research at Boston University, "There's no such thing as 'not racist,'" in the sense of not possessing any ill will or animosity against other people based on the color of their skin or their national origin or ethnicity. Kendi explains, "The concept of 'not-racism' is really just an act of denial." But more than that, calling yourself a "nonracist" is a form of racism. In fact, most racists deny they are racist, which makes nonracism the most prevalent form of racism.

Essentially, according to Kendi, racism is the absence of antiracism, and antiracism is "the action that must follow both emotional and intellectual awareness of racism." If that isn't circular enough for you, here's Kendi's definition of racist people: "Racist people are people who are expressing racist ideas or are supporting racist policies with their action, or even inaction." Got it? Basically, this is a not-very-interesting or smart way to say, "A racist is anyone I disagree with."

"The only way to undo racism is to consistently identify and describe it—and then dismantle it," says Kendi. Is this something everyone has to do? Not really. As we learned in the other 2019 best-seller about racism, *White Fragility: Why It's So Hard for White People to Talk About Racism,* by Robin DiAngelo, racism is "a white people problem." White people, she explains, live in racism the way a fish lives in water. It is the unacknowledged yet essential condition of life for them, and to have it identified as an unearned privilege causes them to freak out. Hence their "fragility."

She elaborates:

> White privilege is the automatic taken-for-granted advantage be-
> stowed upon white people as a result of living in a society based on
> the premise of white as the human ideal, and that from its founding
> established white advantage as a matter of law and today as a matter
> of policy and practice. And it doesn't matter if you agree with it, if
> you want it, if you even are aware of it, it's twenty-four-seven, three
> sixty-five. And one of the reasons why it's so hard for white people
> to see it, well, there are many reasons, but one is that it serves us
> not to see it. We come to feel entitled to that advantage. We're told
> that we deserve it and that we earned it. And we take great umbrage
> when that is challenged.

Now, let's grant DiAngelo and Kendi the premise that racism remains a big problem in America today. And let's go ahead and say that it's something that white people are responsible for dealing with. There's still a major problem with their argument, which is what logicians and philosophers of science call *unfalsifiability*.

The basic idea is that if you propose a hypothesis, according to the scientific method it has to be testable and repeatable. If you come up with a new medicine, for example, you have to be able to demonstrate that it works, that its success was not due to some other factor, and that anyone else can replicate the experiment. Part of this method, which is key to all progress, is that it be possible for the replication to fail. That is, if the conditions of testing your hypothesis exclude the possibility of disproving it, then the whole matter can be rejected as fallacious.

Both Kendi and DiAngelo run afoul of falsifiability. Kendi says specifically that you can't call yourself a "nonracist," only an "antiracist." You have to accept his premise that racism is the basic state of white consciousness in America, and that being genially accepting of everyone regardless of skin color is a wicked delusion. The only option for white people is to admit to their own racism and pledge allegiance to antiracism. Anything short of that is just denial. DiAngelo similarly argues that when white people are pushed to confront their racism, they respond with anger—hence "white fragility." Once you enter this logical toilet there's no way out but down, because any disagreement with the argument has already been coded as denial.

Their logic is entirely circular. Kendi defines a racist as someone who is not an antiracist, which is another logical fallacy, that of "proving by definition." Basically, you're supposed to be able to say what words mean without using them in your explanation. Saying "'Love' is a loving feeling" doesn't explain what love is.

Similarly, according to DiAngelo, white people live lives "absent of racial stress" because they "enjoy a deeply internalized, largely unconscious sense of racial belonging." This fish-in-water scenario means that white people are essentially stunted, which is why they exist "in a state in which even a minimum amount of racial stress becomes intolerable." When confronted, their defensiveness triggers "emotions such as anger, fear, and guilt, and behaviors such as argumentation, silence, and leaving the stress-inducing situation. These behaviors, in turn, function to reinstate white racial equilibrium."

Ever been in an argument with someone who is passive-aggressive and who insists that your every response—or lack of response—is an overreaction? *Don't interrupt! Why are you frowning? Was that a sigh? I notice you haven't responded in a while.* That's what reading *White Fragility* is like.

To their minor credit, Kendi, DiAngelo, and Hannah-Jones don't say that individual white people should necessarily be punished for their blood guilt. If they embrace antiracism, swear to renounce white privilege, and "dismantle" racism in all its effects, then maybe they will go to atheist heaven.

But how do we "dismantle" racism? The overarching point that the race industry wants to make is that it doesn't really much matter what individuals say or do. As DiAngelo explains,

> The disavowal of race as an organizing factor, both of individual white consciousness and the institutions of society at large, is necessary to support current structures of capitalism and domination, for without it, the correlation between the distribution of social resources and unearned white privilege would be evident. The existence of structural inequality undermines the claim that privilege is simply a reflection of hard work and virtue.

The problem is not that some white person may make an offensive remark to a black person. The problem is that the "institutions of society at large" that support "capitalism and domination" are structured around "unearned white privilege." White people like to imagine that their material success—no matter how marginal it might be—is a "reflection of hard work and virtue." But in reality, it is all stolen and undeserved.

Here we get to the heart of the matter. "Structural racism," or "institutional racism," is the real problem, and the only solution is a complete reordering of society from top to bottom. The entire project is indistinguishable from old-fashioned communism, except that you can substitute "black" for "worker." The antiracist project aims to "help" and "empower" nonwhites just as the communists wanted to create a "worker's paradise." But in both cases, the beneficiaries of the help are just a tool for the revolutionaries to seize power.

Now, many people have noticed that the new definition of racism doesn't mesh very well with the definition of racism that most of us were taught. The most famous adage of the twentieth century—up there with "Do unto others as you would have them do unto you"—is probably Martin Luther King Jr.'s admonition to judge people "not by the color of their skin, but by the content of their character."

King's words are justifiably famous. He understood that a just and right society begins with the recognition between individuals of their common humanity. And his motto is universally applicable: everyone should judge each other by the content of their character.

That's probably why the woke Left loathes King and rolls its eyes whenever some naïve soul quotes him. The Left doesn't want racism to be a question of individual conscience and fellow-feeling, and they don't want it to be something that anyone can express. As DiAngelo says, racism is not a question of not saying mean things to black people. True antiracism is about massive wealth distribution, jobs programs that they control, indoctrination of your children, and a complete reevaluation of American values. And racism is not something that impacts white people, because that would make the Left's restructuring of society along racial lines unnecessarily complicated.

## EQUITY, NOT EQUALITY

*Equity* is a funny word, as the wokesters use it. It sounds a lot like *equality* but actually means the exact opposite. When we talk about equality in society, we usually mean that everyone should get an equal shot—equality of opportunity. Everyone should have access to education and training. Everyone should get treated fairly when it comes to getting a bank loan or getting a job. That's why we instituted antidiscrimination laws almost six decades ago, in order to ensure that people could get equal treatment before the law. It's why teams switch sides at halftime, to ensure that everyone is playing on a level field. Equality is the essence of the American way.

Equity is something else. Equity means taking into consideration the fact that not everybody gets an equal shot at opportunity, for a variety of reasons, and taking affirmative steps to level not just the playing field, but (to mix sports metaphors) the starting line. It means giving historically underrepresented groups a boost in admissions or hiring, even if that means penalizing other groups that may, for reasons of unearned privilege, have a more merit-based claim to the societal goods.

According to Ibram X. Kendi, "Racial inequity is evidence of racist policy and the different racial groups are equals." Equity means equality of outcome, in other words. If a group of people take a test, and there is a difference in how people of different races perform on it, that means definitively that the test is racist, or some policy leading up to the taking of the test is racist. In either case, Kendi would like to see an antiracist amendment to the Constitution that would ban "racial inequity over a certain threshold, as well as racist ideas by public officials."

That sounds extreme, but it's really not so far off from how universities, corporations, and government offices are currently conducting themselves—ahead of any laws or regulations requiring them to do so, I might add. Suddenly, every institution in America has a "Diversity, Equity, and Inclusion" (DEI) office—staffed by highly paid professionals in the field of grievance—charged with ensuring that "inequity," or merit, is suppressed in professional hiring, advancement, and compensation.

Equity is meant to eliminate "disparate impact," which is the tendency of different groups to do different things and excel in different ways. Economist Thomas Sowell has analyzed the ways in which different ethnic or national groups all over the world have, for a variety of reasons pertaining to culture, family, caste, or history, gravitated toward specific trades or professions. This "sorting" is occasionally the result of discrimination but occurs naturally in free societies.

For example, Nigerians and West Indians who immigrate to the United States make more money and are better educated than most white Americans, as do their American-born children, because they bring with them a culture of hard work and place a high value on school. Yet these same populations are black, so how can it be that they succeed in a nation shot through with white supremacist racism?

Similarly, we hear a lot about the "pay gap" between men and women. Women, we are told, only make 75 cents for every dollar a man makes. But these reports never compare like-with-like. If these studies are honest and compare men and women with equal amounts of school, training, and experience, they invariably find that the pay gap shrinks to the point that it is invisible or negligible.

The logic of disparate impact, as Kendi explains, is that any difference is evidence of racism. This is taken to absurd conclusions.

Professional baseball, we are told, has a problem: black Americans, who make up about 13 percent of the general population, are underrepresented in Major League Baseball, where only 7 percent of the roster is black. Seventy-five years after Jackie Robinson broke the color line, we are told, baseball has yet to fulfill its promise as America's pastime.

Of course, 11 percent of the MLB is from the Dominican Republic, and most of them are either black or otherwise nonwhite, so the MLB is hardly excluding nonwhite players. But about 75 percent of professional basketball players and 58 percent of the National Football League are black. Is that a problem? Overrepresentation in one area demands, by the law of averages, underrepresentation somewhere else.

In any case, all discussion of disparate impact, equity, structural racism, etc., is pointed toward one main idea: that America is a white supremacist authoritarian state, and white Americans are in a stupor of denial about it because the current state of affairs protects their ill-gotten riches. According to the 1619 Project, among many other leftist misreadings of history, all of the wealth of America was generated by the unpaid labor of black slaves, which demands repayment in the form of reparations. White people owe black people trillions upon trillions of dollars—essentially, everything.

Certainly slaves were mistreated and their forced labor benefited their owners. However, economically speaking, the argument that slavery created all the wealth of America doesn't make much sense. For one thing, most of labor throughout history has been performed by slaves, and while it is true that American slavery had certain unique features in that it was defined so specifically by race, the fact that they labored was not especially unique.

Moreover, as everyone knows, the slave states were much poorer than the North, in large part because the institution of slavery was a negative incentive to industrialize the region. And the Civil War, famously, destroyed the South and all its wealth. Also, if slavery was such a source of riches to the United States, we would expect that the decades following the abolition of slavery would have been a time of economic depression, as the country tried to figure out how to retool itself. But, to the contrary, the last third of the nineteenth century saw a massive expansion of the economy, despite the lack of slaves to exploit.

Plus, it's not like we haven't been over all this before. Since 1964, when Lyndon Johnson announced the War on Poverty, the federal government has expended at least $30 trillion on anti-poverty programs, disproportionately targeting black Americans. Affirmative action programs have been in place for half a century. Fair housing, Title I funding for schools with poor children, multiple rounds of assistance to black farmers who sued because they missed out on earlier lawsuits, Section 8 vouchers . . . all of this has disproportionately aided black Americans. I'm not against helping poor people, but it is ridiculous to pretend that we are starting in Year Zero.[1]

As America moves incrementally toward a reparations scheme, which more and more public figures and prestige media outlets endorse each year, expect to hear more about historical black contributions to American wealth and new ways in which blacks were robbed of their patrimony. For example, New York State recently legalized marijuana. As part of the franchising process—deciding who will get licenses to run legal marijuana businesses—the state has decided to prioritize people with marijuana-related criminal records.

The idea, according to the advocates of this measure, is that "black and brown" people were innovators, risking their freedom to bring their entrepreneurial spirit to the sale of the illicit weed. As such, giving them the first crack at the legal opportunity is only fair. The state is even going to kick in $200 million to help "social equity applicants" rent storefronts, buy office and security equipment, and help smooth their transition from ex-convict to legitimate businessman.

Giving marijuana licenses to former drug dealers sounds pretty absurd, but it's the height of rational policy-making compared to some of the lunacy that has been emanating from the racial equity complex, especially after the insanity that followed in the wake of the George Floyd riots. In the battle to uproot racism from America, activists and visionaries refused to rest. They searched high and low, and found offending (and offensive) signs and symbols everywhere they looked—unsurprisingly, because they see it everywhere.

Everyone knows that math skills and reading proficiency are key to success in a modern society like ours. And getting everyone up to speed should be a top priority. Unfortunately, our school system has done a poor job in regard to black youth, who consistently underperform their white and Asian schoolmates on standardized tests that measure basic competency. Rather than try to figure out what the problem is—whether the schools are failing, or if there is a cultural bias among some communities against taking school seriously—our woke system of public education, dominated by the hard-left teachers' unions, wants to throw out standards of merit.

Any racial disparity must be the fault of a racist policy. So if black kids aren't doing well on a test—throw out the test. This is the answer that school systems are increasingly embracing around the country. New York City, the largest school system in the nation—with over one million students—made plans under the previous administration to eliminate Gifted & Talented programs and end "tracking" of students, which is supposedly discriminatory.

School systems around the country are deemphasizing advanced math classes because black students don't do so well in them. For instance, white third graders achieved proficiency on standardized math tests at four times the rate of their black classmates. In response, teachers are rejecting the old standards. As *USA Today* reported in December 2021:

> Algebra classes taught by Nadine Ebri look different than the ones you probably took in school. Students practice equations through singing, dancing and drawing. Activities are sculpted around their hobbies and interests: anime, gaming, Minecraft. Problem-solving is a team sport, rather than an individual sprint to the right answer.

I am all in favor of teamwork. As a Marine pilot I learned the importance of teams working together toward a common goal. There was no question that I needed the maintenance and repair crew, the ordnance teams, the parachute riggers, and the hundreds of other personnel who worked together to make our missions successful. But at the end of the day, I was in the pilot's seat and had to rely on myself and my training to fly and land the plane. The idea that "singing, dancing and drawing" are going to prepare kids to excel in an advanced economy is a total fantasy.

It almost sounds as if the people behind this curriculum don't want to produce a new generation of doctors, researchers, engineers, and mechanics—people who know how to think on their feet and apply their knowledge skills to the resolution of real problems. Maybe what they really want is a society of grown-up kindergartners, who think that the answer to every thorny question is just a matter of circle time, followed by finger-painting a mural, and then a nap. A society inhabited by helpless adult toddlers would be pliable, and happy to follow the orders of the ruling class.

The problem with black achievement in math, it turns out, isn't a question of test scores, grades, or performance. The problem is that by talking about this issue—even suggesting it exists—we are imposing mental hindrances on black students by making them think that they are naturally bad at math. "In practice, whiteness can create a self-fulfilling prophecy" when it comes to math education, according to Dan Battey of Rutgers University.

"Equity for Black learners in mathematics education," explains Danny Martin, a professor at the University of Illinois at Chicago, "is a delusion rooted in the fictions of white imaginaries, contingent on appealing to white logics and sensitivities, and characterized at best by incremental changes that do little to threaten the maintenance of racial hierarchies inside or outside of mathematics education."[2]

I am not sure what "white logics" are, but I guess it's not good. Funny, I always thought that logic proceeded by rational steps and applied generally to everybody. But apparently not.

Replacing the old ways of doing white supremacist math is "A Pathway to Equitable Math Instruction," a team backed by Microsoft cofounder Bill Gates and working in conjunction with the entire California public schools administrator-teacher-educrat establishment. "*A Pathway to Equitable Math Instruction* is an integrated approach to mathematics that centers Black, Latinx, and Multilingual students in grades 6–8, addresses barriers to math equity, and aligns instruction to grade-level priority standards," runs the mission statement.[3]

The Pathway will "develop an anti-racist math practice" by "Centering Ethnomathematics." The guidebook, which "while primarily for math educators . . . advocates for a collective approach to dismantling white supremacy," explains how your average math teacher in an average California junior high school classroom can seek to overturn American society by teaching their students how math is "resistance":

- Recognize the ways that communities of color engage in mathematics and problem solving in their everyday lives.
- Teach that mathematics can help solve problems affecting students' communities. Model the use of math as a solution to their immediate problems, needs, or desires.

- Identify and challenge the ways that math is used to uphold capitalist, imperialist, and racist views.
- Teach the value of math as both an abstract concept and as a useful everyday tool.
- Expose students to examples of people who have used math as resistance. Provide learning opportunities that use math as resistance.

You think it's a problem that kids can't do long division or calculate a tip? Maybe *you're* the problem, mister!

## NEXT STOP, PRISON!

Teaching antiracism is one thing. But what's a teacher to do when Johnny not only can't read but can't stop beating up his classmates? "Culturally responsive discipline" is the next new thing in the schools. It turns out that black and Latino kids receive (supposedly) disproportionately harsh punishment, and that when white kids do the same misdeeds, their discipline is comparatively light. This dynamic has created the "school-to-prison pipeline."

Researchers from Harvard University, Boston University, and the University of Colorado at Boulder conducted a survey, the findings of which show "that early censure of school misbehavior causes increases in adult crime—that there is, in fact, a school-to-prison pipeline," as they wrote on *Education Next*. "Any effort to maintain safe and orderly school climates must take into account the clear and negative consequences of exclusionary discipline practices for young students, and especially young students of color, which last well into adulthood."

The study found that students who attend schools with high suspension rates are more likely to be arrested and jailed as adults, and this holds especially true for black and Latino boys. Of course, it might also mean that the sort of people who grow up to be criminals also happened to be troublemakers when they were younger. Assuming that being suspended from school is the cause of your problems later in life seems like a radical confusion of cause and effect.

So part of the answer is to stop suspending kids, or at least to mete out discipline in a culturally responsive manner. What does that mean, exactly? According to the Southern Poverty Law Center's "Teaching Tolerance" initiative, teachers need to approach "defiant" students with a focus on their own attitudes and preconceptions. "What do I know about my students' families and cultures? Am I using my role as a teacher to advocate for a shift away from zero-tolerance? Which do I do more often: praise my students or discipline them?"[4]

At the end of this long, dark road, we wind up with the predictable conclusion that discipline should be *equitized*. Equality of discipline would mean that everybody gets the same punishment for the same infraction. But the new mode of culturally responsive discipline would seek to have the same rate of suspension or other measures, not according to what was done, but according to the race of the perpetrator.

## EMOJIS ARE RACIST

America has gone completely race-crazy. We see this all the time. Did you know that using the default yellow "thumbs-up" or "wave" emoji in texting is racist? Well, it is. White people use it to hide their whiteness and pretend that they inhabit a neutral racial space. According to NPR, use of the yellow emoji is a way to deny the reality of white privilege.

After the George Floyd "racial reckoning," corporate America decided to tackle its role in fostering white supremacy. Vener-

able brands that used nonwhite characters in their logos realized that they were exploiting marginalized people for profit, and
appropriating their images without regard for the culture they
were robbing. To atone for this problematic use of iconography,
Quaker/PepsiCo changed the name of Aunt Jemima pancake mix
and syrup to Pearl Milling Company, and removed the image of
a black woman that had identified the product for more than a
century. Hours later, Mars Inc. announced similar changes to its
Uncle Ben's rice brand. Land O'Lakes butter removed the Indian
woman from its packaging, too. The chef on the Cream of Wheat
box—gone.

Maybe that all makes sense. Were black and Native people
troubled by the imagery? I never heard about it, but to be honest, I
wasn't paying a lot of attention to the question. But the end result
of the corporate cleansing is that the grocery aisles of America
now display no nonwhite faces on the packaging. We still have the
Quaker Oats guy, and Betty Crocker, and Colonel Sanders and Little Debbie and a host of other white representations selling America its packaged food. So isn't that kind of . . . racist? I expect in
another few years we will read studies proving that black children
feel worse after a trip to the supermarket, because there are no
packages that "look like them," to use the language of inclusion.

The proof that our society is reaching a kind of boiling point of
racial lunacy is the concept of "microaggressions." The idea is that
white supremacy and institutionalized racism have become so totalizing that even ostensibly polite or neutral interactions are tainted
by it. Microaggressions are tiny, passive-aggressive instances of racism that white people inflict on nonwhites all day long, and the
aggregate effect is traumatizing and horrible.

What are some examples of microaggressions? According to the
University of California, Santa Cruz, asking someone where they
are from or where they were born sends the message "You are not a

true American." Asserting that one "doesn't believe in race" is a way of "denying the individual as a racial/cultural being." If a woman shifts her pocketbook when a black person gets on the elevator, that's microaggressive, and so is asking a black woman a question about her hair.

Even major pharmaceutical corporations are worried about microaggressions. According to the Pfizer website, "While a micro-aggression may seem harmless, a lifetime of microaggressions can be quite devastating to a person's mental health. . . . Research con-tinues to show that racism and discrimination contribute to poor health among minorities and people of color, resulting in increased rates of depression, prolonged stress and trauma, anxiety, even heart disease and type 2 diabetes." Maybe Pfizer is preparing a vaccine to prevent microaggressions.

Here's the thing about microaggressions that is at once blind-ingly obvious and totally mysterious: in a truly racist society, nobody would ever talk about microaggressions because there would be so much actual macroaggression going on that little comments or gestures would be beneath notice. If black people were constantly getting killed by whites—as used to happen in the South, where there was an average of a lynching each week—or if blacks were denied equal access to public accommodations like restaurants and airplanes, then nobody would be talking about how a shop clerk gave them a funny look. It's only because our society has become so miraculously free of actual racism that the space is open for liars and hustlers to concoct a fiction of ongoing white supremacy based on fleeting feelings of neurotic paranoia.

# CHAPTER FOUR

## Obama's Divided America

IT SHOULD BE UTTERLY CLEAR that America has gone off the deep end regarding race. After Will Smith walked onstage at the Oscars and slapped presenter Chris Rock for making a mild, lame joke about Smith's wife, Jada Pinkett Smith, we were forced to endure hundreds of hours of discussion and analysis of this clash. The most bizarre comment came from Eisa Nefertari Ulen, a professor at Hunter College in Manhattan, who appeared on *PBS NewsHour* to explain:

I think that any time we witness violence, we need to understand that from a place where we recognize the emotional and psychological state that's driving this physical response to a trigger.

And Will Smith was definitely triggered that night. But I think, in the broader context of American society, we need to understand what was happening there, it's really rooted and steeped in a 400-year commitment to Black erasure, Black marginalization, Black silencing, and the stereotyping of Black people.

Will Smith has been a superstar since he was a teenager. He is worth an estimated $350 million. He probably thinks having to fly first class in a commercial airplane as opposed to taking a private jet is a demonstration of humility, if not actual privation. A few minutes after striking Chris Rock, he won the Best Actor Oscar. If that's "Black erasure, Black marginalization, Black silencing," America has a funny way of showing it.

If all the race lunacy that I laid out in the previous chapter was limited to entitled actors sobbing about how misunderstood they are, or office workers having to sit through interminable DEI lectures, or confused op-eds mangling U.S. history, we could probably manage to laugh it off. But unfortunately, the "racial reckoning" has extraordinarily malign real-world consequences, and is directly connected to the disastrous public safety climate America has found itself in.

## OBAMA'S PROMISE

To understand how things unfolded, we have to understand the central role that Barack Obama has played in America over the last fifteen years. As our first black president, Obama came to power bearing enormous, perhaps impossible, hopes that he would unify the country. Many people harkened to his sensible, centrist message and his apparent willingness to speak some hard truths about black culture to the only people who could do something about it. Many whites, including me, were heartened by the possibility that Obama embodied the dream of an America that could finally go beyond race.

Obama's famous Father's Day speech in June 2008—after he had clinched enough delegates to secure the Democratic nomination for the presidency—was delivered to the congregants of the Apostolic Church of God on Chicago's South Side, not far from where he lived. He made some bold statements about the need for black fathers to step up and play an active role in their kids' lives. "If we are honest with ourselves," said the junior senator from Illinois, "we'll admit that what too many fathers also are is missing—missing from too many lives and too many homes. They have abandoned their responsibilities, acting like boys instead of men. And the foundations of our families are weaker because of it."[1]

These were strong words, and they received significant backlash from liberals who sniffed that Obama was "blaming the victim." But the United States leads the world in single-parent families, which virtually all sociologists and observers agree is a major predictor of negative life outcomes for children raised in that environment. No one who is honest or who isn't paid to say so will contend that a single mother can raise children, especially boys, just as capably without their father around. Study after study has demonstrated that the stability afforded by a two-parent home radically improves a child's life chances. Of course, the material stability is important, but the spiritual and moral guidance that a father provides as a manly role model is vital to helping kids grow up with a sense of purpose, drive, and discipline.

Obama did not pull punches, and his words are worth quoting at length, because of how true they were then, and how true they remain today:

You and I know how true this is in the African American community. We know that more than half of all black children live in single-parent households, a number that has doubled—

doubled—since we were children. We know the statistics—that children who grow up without a father are five times more likely to live in poverty and commit crime, nine times more likely to drop out of schools, and twenty times more likely to end up in prison. They are more likely to have behavioral problems, or run away from home or become teenage parents themselves. And the foundations of our community are weaker because of it.

Obama did not put the blame—as so many tend to do—on the failings of society, but squarely addressed black fathers, telling them that they needed not just to be around, but to serve as strong, positive models of engaged, loving parents:

We need fathers to realize that responsibility does not end at conception. We need them to realize that what makes you a man is not the ability to have a child—it's the courage to raise one. . . . It's a wonderful thing if you are married and living in a home with your children, but don't just sit in the house and watch *SportsCenter* all weekend long. That's why so many children are growing up in front of the television. As fathers and parents, we've got to spend more time with them, and help them with their homework, and replace the video game or the remote control with a book once in a while.

The churchgoers in Obama's audience were accustomed to this kind of sermonizing, but many Americans—both black and white—were taken aback by what sounded like the sort of thing that conservatives usually say. Some critics accused Obama of "pathologizing" black men and blaming them for social conditions that were the result of decades of "disinvestment" in their communities. Jesse Jackson was caught on a Fox News hot mike telling a fellow panelist that Obama was "talking down to black people," and that he wanted to "cut his nuts off."

Political observers noted that Obama was "triangulating" ahead of the election, signaling to white centrists that, though his skin was black, he wasn't buying all the liberal pap about black culture and victimhood that America is used to hearing from Democrats, especially black Democrats. Hearing a black senator tell a black audience not to feed their children "cold Popeyes" for breakfast was shocking; if a white politician made remarks like that, his career would certainly have ended. But Obama could get away with calling out black cultural dysfunction without being accused of being a racist or currying favor with racists in his party. And even if white centrists understood that Obama's harsh language was part of his campaign strategy, it was still a good signal that he was willing to stake his credibility on the goal of getting the black underclass to start cleaning up its act. Obama won the election handily, and was hailed as our first "postracial president," the one who would finally unite the great American divide.

## GOING BACK ON HIS PROMISE

The honeymoon ended quickly. In July 2009, Harvard professor Henry Louis Gates Jr. got locked out of his house in Cambridge, Massachusetts, and was trying to force his door open with the help of his cabdriver. A witness called the police, who responded to what sounded like a burglary. Details are vague, but Gates apparently argued vigorously with Sergeant James Crowley, possibly refusing to show that he lived at the address. In any event, he was arrested and charged with disorderly conduct. The charges were later dropped.

This was the sort of local matter that, absent the celebrity of the arrestee, would have drawn zero attention. Even after it made the news, however, there was little reason for President Obama to opine on the matter. But when he was asked about it, Obama, who loves to hear himself speak, weighed in anyway, saying,

> I don't know, not having been there and not seeing all the facts, what role race played in that. But I think it's fair to say, number one, any of us would be pretty angry; number two, that the Cambridge police acted stupidly in arresting somebody when there was already proof that they were in their own home, and, number three, what I think we know separate and apart from this incident is that there's a long history in this country of African Americans and Latinos being stopped by law enforcement disproportionately.

Obama first admitted he didn't know the facts of the case or that race played any role in it. But that didn't stop him from saying that Crowley acted "stupidly," and then strongly implying that his actions were motivated by racial stereotyping, if not outright animus. It must be stressed that Henry Louis Gates never alleged Sergeant Crowley said anything about race, nor that he was treated abusively or roughly by him. The narrative about race that blew up around the story was entirely imported into it, because the facts that weren't "separate and apart from this incident" said nothing about race or racism.

Obama raised to public consciousness the idea that the "long history in this country of African Americans and Latinos being stopped by law enforcement disproportionately" means that these stops are unfair. This relates to the question of *equity* that I talked about in the last chapter. If blacks and Latinos are indeed stopped by law enforcement out of proportion to their numbers, what true inferences can be made from this statement? Many people, both in 2009 and today, would say that it's plain evidence that policing in America is racist. Why else would blacks be stopped more frequently if it weren't the case that the police are picking on them?

But suppose it's the case that blacks and Latinos get stopped by the police more frequently because they live in areas with more crime? This happens to be true, and it's not a question of police hanging out in their neighborhoods waiting to arrest the first nonwhite they see drop a candy wrapper on the sidewalk. Emergency 911 calls drive police response rates, and those come predominantly from black and Latino callers in black and Latino neighborhoods, which in fact do have higher rates of crime than whiter neighborhoods. And I am talking about serious crime, not spitting on Sundays.

President Obama didn't bother to make these distinctions, instead hitting on a message whose resonance would be steadily amplified over the next decade: police "stupidly" behave in a racist manner, frequently and illegitimately arresting people for no good reason. This was a significant change in how presidents talk about the police. It is hard to recall any time in history when a sitting president would bother to discuss a local, minor arrest and so strongly criticize the cops for doing their job.

Police around the country were outraged by Obama's comments, which they rightly saw as authorizing and legitimating an ugly point of view commonly held by elements of American underclass society, and among members of the liberal elite in academia and the media. Spreading the idea that police are stupid and racist is common among radical local politicians and some extremist members of Congress, but many normal, law-abiding people were dismayed to hear this kind of poison coming from the White House. In his 2020 memoir, A Promised Land, Obama wrote that internal polling indicated that his comments caused a bigger drop in white support for his administration than any other episode in his presidency. Obama also revealed in his memoir that black members of his staff and many black supporters were annoyed that he was forced to "bend over backwards" to be evenhanded in his treatment of the police officer. The nation's first black president, Obama implies, shouldn't have to kowtow to a white cop who dared question a Harvard professor.

But having been elected to be president of racial healing, Obama apparently decided to shift gears, especially after the 2010 midterm elections, which were devastating for the Democrats, who lost the House and the Senate, as well as six governors and twenty legislative chambers. It was a crushing, humiliating defeat for Obama, who began to move away from his message of unity and toward the politics of racial division.

## SONS OF OBAMA

The death of Trayvon Martin in 2012 quickly became a flashpoint around the country. Martin was a seventeen-year-old visiting his father and his father's girlfriend at her house in Sanford, Florida. After buying some snacks, he was wandering around the community, which had a big problem with burglaries and break-ins; cops were called an average of once daily to respond to crimes at the Retreat at Twin Lakes, a working-class, mixed-race housing development.

A longtime resident, George Zimmerman, had been selected to run a Neighborhood Watch program. Seeing Martin skulking around, peering into windows, Zimmerman called the cops and told them that there was a suspicious person lurking about. It's unclear precisely how the events unfolded, but Martin apparently confronted Zimmerman and began beating him up. Zimmerman, who was licensed to carry a firearm, wound up shooting the teenager.

Police who arrived on the scene found Martin dead on the

ground, and Zimmerman bleeding from his face and the back of his head. Ascertaining that Martin had been pounding Zimmerman's head against the pavement, the cops, the police chief, and the local prosecutor all accepted his claim of self-defense and insistence that Martin had been the aggressor in the conflict.

The death of Trayvon Martin was soon elevated to national importance, as soon as the media and race hustlers like Benjamin Crump and Al Sharpton got hold of it. The case was immediately turned into a story of a snarling white vigilante chasing down a harmless black teenager walking the streets of an elite, gated community. It was widely called a "lynching." Martin was described in angelic terms, and the bag of candy he was carrying became like a sacred symbol of his innocence. Skittles wrappers became an icon of his martyrdom. Angelic pictures of Martin from when he was about twelve years old were widely disseminated, and he was described as an honor student who was "majoring in cheerfulness," standing about five-foot-nine, versus George Zimmerman, "terrifying—larger, older, carrying a weapon." According to the *Washington Post*, "Dead children, dead kids, often carry with them the burden of our outsize hopes. 'He could have been president,' one commentator noted. He could have been an astronaut. Hope can cast shadows as massive and false as those cast by fear."

In fact, Martin was estimated by his mother to be six-foot-two, and had been recently suspended from school three times, for drugs, graffiti, and suspicion of burglary. His social media was filled with references to drugs, guns, and sexual aggression. Zimmerman, who was actually five-foot-eight, was widely condemned as a racist "white Hispanic," though he is visibly nonwhite, and dozens of people who knew him well came forward to say that he never displayed any racial prejudice whatsoever.

The media embraced the narrative that the killing of Trayvon

Martin was a case of racial profiling, white vigilantism, and another instance in America's long history of murderous hate against black people. Constant comparisons were made between the death of Martin and the 1955 murder of Emmett Till, a black teenager from Chicago who was killed while visiting family in Mississippi, after he allegedly sexually harassed a young white woman. The killing of Till became a national scandal, especially after the acquittal of his suspected murderers in a trial that was widely believed to be slanted in favor of the defense.

Noted civil rights leader, popularizer of the term *African American* instead of *black*, and erstwhile presidential candidate Jesse Jackson was among the first to compare Martin to Till. "We mourn Trayvon Martin, the young African American who, armed only with candy and a soft drink, was shot dead for the offense of 'walking while black,'" wrote Jackson in late March 2012. "George Zimmerman, the vigilante who shot him, has not been arrested, apparently protected by Florida's 'Stand Your Ground' law, which 'authorizes' anyone to shoot someone whom he or she feels is threatening."

Florida's "Stand Your Ground" law means that people don't have a "duty to retreat" if they feel threatened, but are allowed to use force to defend themselves. After the Trayvon Martin killing, many pointed to the alleged absurdity of these laws, implying that they provided white southern racists a "fire at will" license to kill black people if they felt obscurely threatened by them. In fact, Stand Your Ground laws provide no such blanket immunity, and there is no racial implication to their application in the real world. Moreover, George Zimmerman did not appeal to Stand Your Ground in his defense—he didn't have to, because Trayvon Martin was savagely beating him up when he got his gun out and shot him, in a simple use of force in self-defense.

This annoying phrase "X-ing while black," incidentally, has

become a cliché, but in 2012 it still sounded fresh and shocking. "Driving while black," "shopping while black," "jogging while black" . . . any black person who gets in trouble can make the claim that they were merely minding their own business when they were sucked into the vortex of racial brutality that supposedly defines American history and continues to drag innocent people into its whirlpool.

Jackson continued, pronouncing, "Now we must choose: We will decide if Trayvon Martin's death is a moment, or becomes the spark for a movement. We can't bring him back. But we can make his voice louder in death than it could be in his short life. Emmett Till's murder sparked a movement. After he was brutally beaten, his mother put him in an open casket to show the horror that he had endured. Although he was crucified as a warning to others who might demand freedom, his murder gave some the courage to join the civil rights movement."

The case of Emmett Till remains shrouded in some mystery about what really happened. He appears to have sexually harassed, and probably assaulted, Carolyn Bryant, but it's unquestionable that the men who killed the teenager in 1955 were not being threatened by him. It was certainly a revenge killing and a lynching. Such qualifying factors did not enter the Martin case at all. Linking Martin—a marginally delinquent youth who seemed to aspire to becoming a gangster—to one of the martyrs of the civil rights movement was grotesque, but also established a new model for representing these sorts of cases to the public.

Barack Obama—facing a tight campaign for reelection later that year—decided to step directly into another local police blotter matter, legitimizing and amplifying the atmosphere of racial hostility around it. In an unrelated press conference a few weeks after Zimmerman killed Martin, the president spoke out about the case, inflaming tensions and passions. "When I think about this boy, I think about my own kids, and I think every parent in America should be able to understand why it is absolutely imperative that we investigate every aspect of this," said Obama, who then added his famously fatuous, inflammatory, and unnecessary statement, "If I had a son he would look like Trayvon."

A year later, Zimmerman was acquitted of charges of murder. This was no surprise: political pressure had led the prosecutors to overcharge Zimmerman. Violent protests broke out across the country. In Mississippi, a white jogger was kidnapped by black motorists, who beat him badly, telling him, "This is for Trayvon." In Toledo, Ohio, an elderly man was beaten almost to death by six black juveniles who also yelled, "This is for Trayvon!" Los Angeles saw days of rioting, and a news crew was set upon and beaten by a mob.

Obama spoke up again. "You know," he said, "when Trayvon Martin was first shot, I said that this could have been my son. Another way of saying that is Trayvon Martin could have been me, thirty-five years ago." Could it really have been him? Did Obama lurk around neighborhoods, peering into windows? Did he aggressively confront neighborhood watchmen, and pummel them on the ground, raining down punches on their faces?

What's most pernicious about Obama's comments is his repetition of the idea that his son "would look like" Trayvon Martin, or that Trayvon Martin "could have been" Obama. In our society it is considered the height of disrespect to imply that people of the same race "all look alike." But Obama insisted just the opposite. He reduced his and Martin's identities to their skin color, demanding that everyone participate in the fiction that American society is so mired in reductive stupidity that we refuse to look at anyone past the most superficial element of racial presentation. Barack Obama went to Ivy League schools, became a U.S. senator, and then was elected president, but according to what has become the dominant narrative among the Left, it is only by the grace of God that he isn't shot dead every day by white vigilantes out for blood.

## HOW DARE YOU?

Michelle Obama has made similar remarks. In 2011, the First Lady received some criticism for her love for high fashion and expensive jewelry, so her office arranged for her to go "shopping" at Target, dressed in normal clothes, which a veteran news photographer who was detailed to the White House just happened to be present for. This is the kind of transparent photo op that celebrities regularly engineer to make it look like they're just plain folks, heading out to buy cotton swabs and dish detergent "on special," and nobody took it as anything else.

But a couple of years later, the Obamas gave an interview for *People* magazine about "How We Deal with Our Own Racist Experiences." Michelle Obama recounted that during her trip to Target she was racially targeted by a shopper. "I tell this story—I mean, even as the first lady—during that wonderfully publicized trip I took to Target, not highly disguised, the only person who came up to me in the store was a woman who asked me to help her take something off a shelf. Because she didn't see me as the first lady, she saw me as someone who could help her. Those kinds of things happen in life. So it isn't anything new."

The idea that First Lady Michelle Obama, possibly the most famous woman in America at the time, regularly celebrated for her beauty, style, and physical fitness, attended (no doubt) by a heavy Secret Service unit and a personal entourage, was expected to do menial labor for a Target shopper who saw her only as a black woman and thus a servant is absurd. The whole thing is nonsense. But it's exactly the kind of preposterous nonsense that the Obamas demanded we accept, and which the media continues to demand we accept every time the chronicle of injustice against blacks is extended by some new incident.

## MAKING THE NARRATIVE WORK

George Zimmerman was not a police officer, so in a sense the Trayvon Martin case doesn't fit perfectly within the usual narrative. But it's close enough, since Zimmerman was acting in a kind of auxiliary law enforcement role, so the story was made to fit. The Narrative as it is properly defined involves a (preferably) white police officer who kills a (preferably) black civilian. Ideally, the officer is depraved and vicious, and the victim is totally innocent. As it happens, these criteria are seldom if ever met. But the media keeps trying, doggedly, to find a situation in which a racist white police officer can be found to kill—for no good reason—a black pillar of the community.

I'm not going to belabor the long list of failed efforts to make the Narrative work, but I will run through a few of the more notable cases. In July 2014, a massively obese career criminal named Eric Garner was selling loose cigarettes on Bay Street in Staten Island, in New York City. Local shopkeepers had complained about his presence, and police were detailed to investigate. As officers approached the middle-aged Garner, he indicated that he would not consent to be arrested and insisted that he was being harassed. "This ends today," he said. Garner resisted arrest, and in the process of being detained, during which he was brought to the ground, he went into cardiac arrest. He died on his way to the hospital.

The Garner case resulted in a series of protests around the country. In New York City, members of the City Council interrupted their own meeting to walk outside and block traffic on lower Broadway, lying on the ground while chanting "I can't breathe," which were Garner's last words as the exertion of fighting several police officers initiated an asthma attack. In the end, a grand jury refused to indict the officers involved in Garner's arrest, and the U.S. Department of Justice similarly declined to pursue charges.

A few months later, in Ferguson, Missouri, a teenager named Michael Brown stole a box of cigars from a convenience store by use of force; cameras captured him shoving the owner of the store. A police officer saw Brown walking in the middle of the street a short time later and tried to question him. Initial reports emerged that Brown raised his arms in the air and begged, "Hands up, don't shoot," after which police officer Darren Wilson assassinated the teen in cold blood, for no reason at all.

This case exploded. Protests were held around the country, and riots in Ferguson led to the burning of the city's downtown business district. President Obama (predictably) weighed in and dispatched Attorney General Eric Holder to Ferguson to monitor civil rights violations against rioters and arsonists.

After lengthy investigations by the DOJ, it was determined that nothing about the initial reports of the Michael Brown case was correct. He did not raise his hands and say, "Hands up, don't shoot." He reached into Darren Wilson's car and tried to take his gun, which went off in the car. Brown charged at the officer after being told to stop. It was at that point that he was shot.

## FERGUSON EFFECT

Hostility toward the police intensified around the country starting around this time. Former NYPD commissioner Howard Safir described anti-police sentiment as at a fifty-year high. Crime began to spike, and police, reluctant to pursue crime proactively, adopted a reactive posture vis-à-vis fighting crime, which then continued to rise. This vicious cycle became known as the "Ferguson Effect," and while academic sociologists bicker about whether it's real or not, street cops have no doubt that it's happening. Now that everyone with a cell phone is a photojournalist, every police interaction, no matter how normal or justified, can be taken out of context, edited, and amplified by liberals in the media to promote the narrative that police are violent, racist brutalizers. If you are a cop, are you going to volunteer to leap into a tense situation, knowing that you could be the next to be vilified as a civil rights violator, or will you sit back, "work to rule," and let the brass figure out the next steps?

Shortly after the death of Eric Garner, the new mayor of New York City, Bill de Blasio, organized a "roundtable" on police–community relations. De Blasio put himself at the head of the room, with NYPD commissioner Bill Bratton to one side, but surprised everyone by seating the notorious race-baiter Al Sharpton on his other flank. The message was clear: Al Sharpton, who made his name condemning the police, promoting the Tawana Brawley rape hoax in the late 1980s, egging on violent protests in Brooklyn and Harlem, and defending rapists, thugs, and all sorts of scum, was equal to the city's top cop in the eyes of the mayor.

Sharpton punked the mayor and the NYPD at that meeting, saying that Garner's death was a racially motivated murder. "I heard the commissioner say race wasn't involved," scoffed Sharpton. "We don't know that. How do we assume before an investigation that a policeman with two civil rights violations didn't have race involved? So we gonna prejudge what we want and tell the community to wait on the results?" The image of Sharpton, who had spent the last three decades doing everything he could to poison race relations in New York City, scolding the mayor and police commissioner told

New Yorkers who was really in charge when it came to public safety and law enforcement in Gotham.

## "THE TALK"

Things got even worse a few months later after the grand jury declined to indict Daniel Pantaleo, the officer who pulled Eric Garner to the ground while subduing him. At a press conference, surrounded by black council members and other dignitaries, de Blasio referenced his son. As he never tired of reminding everyone, de Blasio had married a black woman (Chirlane McCray) and had two black children, including his son, Dante, a legitimate honors student who was on his way to Yale University. De Blasio made great hay over the fact that his son was black; in fact, when he ran for president in 2020, he noted during one of the debates that he was the only candidate to have raised "a black son in America."

Speaking about his great disappointment that Pantaleo was not going to face charges—yet, anyway—the mayor compared his son, Dante, to Eric Garner, and the shared danger they faced from the police as black men in America. "Chirlane and I have had to talk to Dante for years about the dangers he may face," he explained, referencing his mixed-race son, whom he characterized as "a good young man, a law-abiding young man, who would never think to do anything wrong." De Blasio continued:

> Yet, because of a history that still hangs over us, the dangers he may face—we've had to literally train him, as families have all over this city for decades, in how to take special care in any encounter he has with the police officers who are there to protect him. . . . So I've had to worry, over the years, Chirlane's had to worry—was Dante safe each night?

This stung the NYPD like a slap in the face. The mayor, who effectively commanded the nation's largest and best police department, was accusing it of targeting his own son for racist abuse. Speaking of the "officers who are there to protect him" was especially pointed, because the entire de Blasio family had twenty-four-hour personal protection from the NYPD. De Blasio was basically saying that his own security team might lash out against his son.

The next few days saw violent protests in New York. Protestors on the Brooklyn Bridge attacked cops, punching and kicking them. One protestor, a poet and professor in the city university system, was charged with dropping a heavy garbage can on two lieutenants, injuring them both. But the real fruit of de Blasio's poisonous harvest was when Ismaaiyl Abdullah Brinsley, a Baltimore criminal, shot his girlfriend before hopping a bus to New York. He posted on Instagram his savage plans, swearing that "I'm putting Wings on Pigs today."

When Brinsley got to Brooklyn he quickly sought out and found a target for his anti-cop rage, shooting and killing Rafael Ramos and Wenjian Liu, two uniformed offices sitting in a patrol car on Myrtle Avenue.

Cops were furious and aggrieved, as they always are when their brothers fall in the line of duty. And they were especially angry at Mayor de Blasio, whom they perceived as having invited the assassination of Liu and Ramos with his inflammatory rhetoric about police violence and his association with Al Sharpton. Cops turned their backs en masse on de Blasio when he went to the hospital where the cops' bodies lay, and later, at their funerals as well.

Leaders like Barack Obama and Bill de Blasio, along with dozens of other politicians around the country, could have worked to cool tempers around this issue. There is always a radical, jumped-up segment of the population that is hot to blame society for any trouble that some scoundrel elects to cause. These types love to scream and holler outside police stations, and throw rocks and bottles—or worse—if they think it could lead to violence and disorder. We should elect leaders who can calm these passions, not roil them up further.

The fact that Obama is black and de Blasio the father of a black son could have actually given them additional legitimacy among people sympathetic to the plight of blacks in America. They could have talked about the essential role that police play in black communities, and pointed to the fact that law-abiding residents of those neighborhoods beg police leaders to send more cops to patrol their streets. Obama and de Blasio could have pointed to the real statistics regarding crime in America—which I will get into in the following chapter—and noted that blacks have disproportionately more interactions with the police because they commit disproportionately more crime than whites, Latinos, and Asians.

Instead, Obama and de Blasio each personalized the unfortunate deaths of two lowlifes, insisted that Trayvon Martin and Eric Garner were virtually members of their own family, and thus implied that they were murdered. And that contributed heavily to anti-police sentiments over the next decade, which would result in more bloodshed.

## OBAMA'S FAVORITE SUBJECT

I will end this chapter about Barack Obama—whom I actually voted for in 2008, imagining like so many others that he would set America on a new unified course where race could fade into the background as we got on with the business of living—with a look at one of his last major speeches about the police and racial prejudice. He gave it at the funeral of five Dallas police officers who were murdered—assassinated, really—on July 7, 2016, during a protest against the police killings of Alton Sterling and Philandro Castile, in Louisiana and Minnesota, in recent days.

The killings of the police officers were carried out by Micah Johnson, a black veteran of the military who had expressed a strong interest in black nationalism and had spoken frequently of wanting to engage in violent confrontations with the police. It's important to note that Johnson was in favor of extreme tactics (killing white people), but his basic beliefs (that white racism made life in America impossible for black people) are actually quite mainstream. The bestseller lists in the *New York Times* are filled with books that Johnson would have agreed with; he just would have said that they need to take the next step.

The murder of the five officers (Lorne Ahrens, Michael Krol, Michael Smith, Brent Thompson, and Patricio "Patrick" Zamarripa) was the deadliest incident for law enforcement in the U.S. since 9/11. The funeral was somber. President Obama gave, unsurprisingly, a lengthy and pompous speech at the memorial service. He used a common rhetorical trick, giving praise with one hand, and then subtly disparaging the subject with the other. "We know that the overwhelming majority of police officers do an incredibly hard and dangerous job fairly and professionally. They are deserving of our respect and not our scorn," he said, almost reluctantly. But he followed up this minor acknowledgment of the cops' sacrifice with a doozy:

> We also know that centuries of racial discrimination—of slavery, and subjugation, and Jim Crow—they didn't simply vanish with the end of lawful segregation. They didn't just stop when Dr. King made a speech, or the Voting Rights Act and the Civil Rights Act were signed. Race relations

have improved dramatically in my lifetime. Those who deny it are dishonoring the struggles that helped us achieve that progress.

But we know—but, America, we know that bias remains. We know it. Whether you are black or white or Hispanic or Asian or Native American or of Middle Eastern descent, we have all seen this bigotry in our own lives at some point. We've heard it at times in our own homes. If we're honest, perhaps we've heard prejudice in our own heads and felt it in our own hearts. We know that. And while some suffer far more under racism's burden, some feel to a far greater extent discrimination's sting. Although most of us do our best to guard against it and teach our children better, none of us is entirely innocent. No institution is entirely immune. And that includes our police departments. We know this.

So at the same time that Obama conceded that the police are generally hardworking professionals, he also insisted that they are shot through with bigotry and function as armed agents of racial repression. Even the most hard-core anti-cop Antifa radicals will probably agree that some cops are okay as individuals. But it's a central premise of the Left that individuals don't matter; only systems do. And the system is totally corrupt.

Obama even went out of his way to praise Alton Sterling, the thirty-seven-year-old Baton Rouge, Louisiana, man whose shooting precipitated the rioting in the first place. Sterling was a violent criminal and a sex offender who was waving a gun around and threatening people who didn't want to buy the CDs he was selling. He resisted arrest and was Tased several times. The police shot him when he was reaching for his gun.

President Obama demanded that we honor the memory of Alton Sterling, attempted cop-killer:

With an open heart, police departments will acknowledge that, just like the rest of us, they are not perfect; that insisting we do better to root out racial bias is not an attack on cops, but an effort to live up to our highest ideals. And I understand these protests— I see them, they can be messy. Sometimes they can be hijacked by an irresponsible few. Police can get hurt. Protestors can get hurt. They can be frustrating.

But even those who dislike the phrase "Black Lives Matter," surely we should be able to hear the pain of Alton Sterling's family. We should—when we hear a friend describe him by saying that "Whatever he cooked, he cooked enough for everybody," that should sound familiar to us, that maybe he wasn't so different than us, so that we can, yes, insist that his life matters.

I'm sorry, but if some dude is waving a gun around and threatening people, then he's pretty much put himself on the "My Life Matters Less" list. Let's get real about this.

If Micah Xavier Johnson hadn't been killed after murdering five Dallas police officers, he probably would have applauded Obama's insistence that Sterling's "life matters." It's amazing that Obama retains so much respect and admiration, even among people who ought to know better. When historians look back at this period they will surely identify Obama as the man who did more than anyone to exploit racial division and cynically use it to promote his personal brand.

# CHAPTER FIVE

## Abolish Society: The Vision of BLM

ACCORDING TO THE BLACK LIVES MATTER movement and to the woke communists who support it, we must abolish the police, prisons, and courts.

I wish this were a broad, simplistic overstatement on my part, but it's not. This is what they call for, loud and clear. If we choose to pretend they don't mean it literally, then the blame will be ours once they have won and turned the nation into a garbage dump.

Listen to the words of Patrisse Cullors, the cofounder and former chairperson of Black Lives Matter. If you have any neighbors or relatives who imagine that supporting BLM is a nice thing to do, like being in favor of Martin Luther King Day, or enjoying *Hamilton*, or opposing the N-word, give them a taste of Cullors's words:

Abolition centers on getting rid of prisons, jails, police, courts and surveillance. Period. How it affects us is so much more than that. Abolition is a social justice movement. . . . No matter what part of social justice is your personal bellwether, the abolition of prisons, jails, police, courts and surveillance must be part of that struggle. . . .

This is not about fixing a broken system. We are not looking for better food or more access to education in prison. We are looking to abolish the entire system. . . .

When we center the abolitionist imagination we are actively opposing the current economy of punishment and dreaming up an economy of care that is grounded in love and compassion for true imagining of public safety—not a public safety that is predicated on the unsafety of Black people. . . . The white supremacist capitalist patriarchy is the lens through which we filter all of our experiences. It has been for all of our lives.

The BLM vision of America and its history is of a vast, racist hellhole. It is completely opposed to the idea of reforming society's problems. For BLM, "reforming society" is a contradiction in terms. They want to level society and start all over.

The BLM vision—which is effectively the vision of the Democrat Party, the mainstream media, and the corporations that gave it billions of dollars—demands total revolution. In their rush to appear virtuous, they have unthinkingly signed up for a radical program that would probably shock their conscience were they to bother reviewing it. Think about what it would mean to get rid of "prisons, jails, police, and courts" and replace them with "reimagined," "community-based justice solutions." Based on my study of similar radical experiments—from Bolshevik Russia to Fidel Castro's Cuba to Pol Pot's Cambodia—I suspect it would look something like a Khmer Rouge–style people's tribunal. Throwing out everything in society with the intention of starting from scratch never works, and just means that somebody will be in charge of telling everyone else what to do—and will blame them when it fails.

Year Zero—everybody line up for rock soup!

## LUXURY MARXISM

BLM was founded by self-identified Marxists. They abhor private property—though that doesn't mean they don't enjoy luxury, of course. Patrisse Cullors made news in 2021 when it emerged that she had personally bought four houses, for herself and her family, at a cost of more than $3 million. Then, in late 2021, Cullors, Alicia Garza, and Melina Abdullah—the original cofounders of BLM— used $6 million of BLM money to buy a California "campus" for use "as a haven, as a safe space" for emotionally exhausted BLM activists.

The Los Angeles "campus" includes a 6,500-square-foot house with multiple bedroom suites, a pool, a soundstage, a bungalow, and parking for twenty cars. The BLM troika have offered a confusing defense of the purchase, arguing simultaneously that it's a conference center where the group can produce media, and a "safe house" for BLM leadership when they receive "credible threats" of violence against them.

Facing criticism about the lack of basic paperwork and reporting that is required of all charitable organizations, Cullors pushed back, saying on a conference call with the media that the "recent attacks" were meant to "distract you and us" from the important work that BLM does. She described the purchase of the California property as a "huge accomplishment," and part of a "long legacy of black people wanting to secure land and property."

Filling out Internal Revenue Service forms, she said, is "triggering" and puts her and her comrades at risk. "This is, like, deeply unsafe. This is literally being weaponized against us, against the

people we work with," Cullors said. "People's morale in an organization is so important. But if their organization and the people in
it are being attacked and scrutinized at everything they do, that
leads to deep burnout. That leads to deep, like, resistance and
trauma."

The abolition of police and courts would entail the abolition of
crime, especially property crime, as a category. And the abolition of
property law would mean nothing less than the abolition of property. Human dignity in the BLM worldview is not based on hard
work, prudence, and the possibility of passing down the fruits of
your labor to your children. On the contrary, BLM hates families,
seeks to destroy the family unit as a capitalistic imposition, and
believes that human dignity is based on receiving basic subsistence
from the government. This is no secret—it's all right in the open in
their manifestos, if anyone cared to check.[1]

"Socialists ignore the side of man that is of the spirit," said Ronald Reagan in 1975, as he was preparing his first run for the presidency. "They can provide shelter, fill your belly with bacon and
beans, treat you when you are ill, all the things that are guaranteed
to a prisoner or a slave." Reagan was telling us something profound
about what people are, and what we exist for. People aren't just
walking stomachs waiting to be organized by our masters into the
proper lines. We are God-created souls who strive, in our own small
way, to achieve distant ideals that remain vital guideposts, even if
they elude our reach.

Crime and punishment are complicated subjects that get people angry very easily. Arguments are buried in deep layers of lies
and myth that have lain unquestioned so long they have solidified
into stone. Getting to the reality of why justice matters for everyone means we have to break through this embedded sediment and
sift it for truth.

I want to explore the key myths surrounding law enforcement

NYPD Officers Rafael Ramos and Wenjian Liu were assassinated
in 2014 by a black supremacist criminal who sought revenge
for the deaths of Eric Garner and Michael Brown.
"I'm putting Wings on Pigs today," he wrote.

New Yorkers were horrified in 1972 when NYPD Officers Gregory
Foster and Rocco Laurie were ambushed and murdered by
members of the Black Liberation Army.

The grieving widows of Officers Laurie and Foster personified the shared agony of all crime victims—of all races—and highlighted the danger of police work in the "bad old days."

When Mayor Bill de Blasio and NYPD Commissioner Bill Bratton announced the decriminalization of marijuana by proudly displaying how much pot would be okay to carry around, they signaled to the criminal element that New York City was on the path to lawlessness.

*Getty Images/Spencer Platt*

President Donald Trump carried a Bible to St. John's Church near the White House to call for calm during the George Floyd riots, but his actions were portrayed as inflammatory by a cynical press.

*AP Photo/Patrick Semansk*

More than 60,000 police officers were injured during the "mostly peaceful protests" of 2020, but only the officers involved in the January 6 riot were treated as heroes by the Democrats and the media.

*Oliver Contreras/*The New York Times *via AP, Pool*

The George Floyd/BLM riots made it normal to hate the police and encouraged people to taunt, ridicule, and attack them.

*Getty Images/Alex Wong*

Young Ray Kelly graduated from the NYPD Academy at the
top of his class in 1966 after serving in Vietnam as a
Marine Corps officer.

Kelly became the first NYPD commissioner to return to the
position when Mayor Michael Bloomberg brought him on in 2002.
*Getty Images/Andrew Burton*

Ray Kelly is the longest-serving police commissioner
in the history of the NYPD. Crime was driven to record low levels
and sixteen terrorist plots were averted during his tenure.

*AP Photo/Louis Lanzano*

A tourist snapped this classic photo of NYPD Officer
Larry DePrimo gifting a homeless man a pair of boots on a
cold night in Times Square in 2012. This image exemplifies
the spirit of service that animates police work.

*Jennifer Foster*

in America. This isn't by any means the final word on the subject. But I like to think that this is something you can use to equip yourself with to see through the propaganda we are drowned in by the fake news media every day. Next time you are at a family gathering and some relative is going on about systemic racism in crime and punishment, these arguments should help you refute their unsubstantiated arguments.

## THE MYTH OF OVERINCARCERATION

A key rationale for defunding the police and abolishing courts of law and jails is rooted in the premise that these institutions are used too much. We hear a great deal about how America "overincarcerates" its population relative to other industrialized democracies, and how we live in an era of "mass incarceration."

It is true that we incarcerate more people than any other country in the world, on a per capita basis. America locks up about 6.4 people for every thousand—that's a huge number of people behind bars. You have to go way down the list to find another country of the sort that we typically like to compare ourselves to as a world leader in economic development, literacy, and culture.[2]

Russia has an incarceration rate about half of ours, along with Turkey and Nicaragua. Iran imprisons Iranians at about one-third the American rate. Mexico is even lower. Canada, which is very much like America in many ways, jails only about one person per thousand. When you get down to places like Germany, Denmark, and Sweden, the incarceration rate falls to around one-tenth of our rate. That is to say, we lock up ten times as many people as Germany and Sweden on a per capita basis.

But to call this "mass incarceration" makes it sound as though we round people up "en masse" and send them to jail for baseless reasons. In the Soviet Union, Stalin would deport whole populations to his Siberian gulags. Nazi Germany sent Jews to concentration camps without any due process or consideration of their guilt or innocence. In many communist countries, people of a particular economic background could be arrested and sent to work on farms in order to "reeducate" them.

Nothing like that has happened in the United States during the so-called era of mass incarceration, which began in the mid-1980s, as violent crime spiked. There was no "mass" arrest of people who were then thrown in jail. There were no sweeps where everyone who was unlucky enough to be outside on a given day in a certain street wound up being carted off to a prison camp. Everyone who was arrested was given due process, told what their constitutional rights were, offered a lawyer, confronted with the evidence against them, and given the opportunity to let a jury hear both sides of the story.

Even to say that America "overincarcerates" people is a matter up for debate. "Over" compared to what? There's a lot of crime in America, and it's gone up sharply since the glorious summer of 2020, when so many marched in honor of black lives. The United States puts a lot of people in prison, but we also have a high crime rate compared to other advanced nations. For instance, our intentional homicide rate of roughly 6.3 per 100,000 population is higher than any European nation except Russia. Japan sees only 0.3 murders for every 100,000 people, and China is around that rate, as well.[3]

Why does the U.S. have so much crime? Guns may be part of the reason. Certainly our country is almost unique in the world in codifying the right to bear arms in its most basic framework of laws. A side effect of legal gun ownership is that criminals have easier access to guns here than they might in countries that restrict guns. Some scholars say that it's more appropriate to compare the United States to other nations in the Americas than to Europe or Asia—

New World countries may have retained the violent spirit of explo-
ration and conquest that characterized their founding, which was
comparatively recent in history.

But there are some surprises regarding comparative crime
statistics, too. For instance, New Zealand, which many Americans imagine to be a paradise, has the highest burglary rate in the
world—perhaps because Kiwi burglars have little concern about
getting shot by an alert and armed homeowner. Sweden leaves us in
the dust when it comes to rape and sexual assault, which is driven
by the Scandinavian country's lax vetting of "rapefugees" from the
third world.[4]

But when it comes to the question of American overincarcera-
tion, consider the fact that, according to the FBI, between 2010 and
2018 the United States averaged about 1.2 million violent "index
crimes" (murder and manslaughter, robbery, rape, and assault) and
8.5 million property "index crimes" (burglary, larceny theft, motor
vehicle theft, and arson) annually. But less than half of all violent
crimes, and fewer than 20 percent of property crimes, are "cleared,"
meaning that most of these crimes go completely unpunished.[5]
Many crimes may have been committed by malefactors who were
arrested and jailed for something else they did, but it's not unrea-
sonable to look at the data and realize that there are millions of people who ought to be in prison but aren't. There is a solid argument
to be made that we *under*-incarcerate.

## WHO'S IN PRISON?

The fact that we have a lot of people in prison is one thing. But the
driving premise of the abolition movement is that blacks are treated
in a disproportionately harsh manner compared to whites. The evidence for this is simple, even obvious, they say. Just look at the statistics on black imprisonment, which show that blacks are in prison

or on parole in numbers in excess of their share of the population. As we learned about the logic of disparate impact, any racial difference in outcome is cold evidence of a racist policy.

In fact, according to a line of thought that used to be considered fringe, but which is now widely accepted throughout academia and the media, the whole point of the prison system in the "age of mass incarceration" is to control the black population. We see this argument in books like Michelle Alexander's *The New Jim Crow*. The main argument that Alexander and the abolitionist movement make is that our whole justice system exists to lock up black men. But this idea is not exclusive to the hard Left. In fact, it's essentially the standard perspective among Democrats and liberals generally.

"Echoes of slavery—and the white supremacy that fueled it—continue to reverberate through the U.S. criminal legal system," explains the venerable, lavishly funded, and eminently mainstream Vera Institute of Justice, a research and policy center that gets hundreds of millions of dollars from the federal government in order to protect illegal immigrants from being deported by the federal government. (Yes, that's just as crazy as it sounds.) "The 13th Amendment," says the Vera Institute, "may have outlawed the enslavement of Black people, but the United States continues to devise new ways to uphold the racist hierarchies that slavery was founded on and to restrict the freedom of the descendants of enslaved people."

We also hear this argument in films like Ava DuVernay's *13th*, which was nominated for an Oscar, won a British Academy Film Award, a Peabody Award, and a New York Film Critics Circle Award, and was named on many 2016 top-ten films lists.

*13th* gets its title from the Thirteenth Amendment to the Constitution, which abolished slavery. The amendment, which was ratified in December 1865, just a few months after the Civil War and the assassination of Abraham Lincoln, was the first time the Constitution had been changed in sixty years, and represented the first major extension of civil rights since the founding of the country. The Thirteenth Amendment was a somber and holy expansion of the principle of liberty and the idea that we truly are all "created equal." The fact that hundreds of thousands of Americans paid for the amendment with their blood and lives is a testament to how it represented a sacred recommitment to the American credo.

But to view the Thirteenth Amendment as an instrument of liberation, according to *13th,* is to sleepwalk through the apparent nightmare that is American history. The main text of the amendment is simple: "Neither slavery nor involuntary servitude, except as a punishment for crime whereof the party shall have been duly convicted, shall exist within the United States, or any place subject to their jurisdiction."

Sounds straightforward enough. But did you catch the loophole? Slavery remains intact, according to the new abolitionists, because prisoners can be made to work, assuming they have been "duly convicted" of a crime. This, according to *13th* and its many fans, proves that the insidious purpose of the Thirteenth Amendment—and the antislavery abolitionists who wrote the text—was to move slavery from "plantation to prison." America is so diabolically evil that even when it frees its slaves, it makes sure to re-enslave them in the fine print.

This perversion of reality is everywhere now. Our schools and newsrooms teem with people whose brains are so warped by resentment, bitterness, and hate that they believe that everything—*everything*—about America that isn't explicitly anti-white is racist and should be wiped clean from the slate of history.

Now, the prison abolitionists do have a point. It is true that blacks are in prison at a higher rate than other races. There can be no getting around the fact that blacks make up around 13 percent of the population of the United States, yet account for between 35 percent and 38 percent of the population of our prisons and jails. But is this really a function of racial bias, or is there another, less sinister reason?

The fact is that black criminals are responsible for a much bigger share of crime than you would assume given the relatively small size of the black population in America. While comprising about 13 percent of the country, black people commit more than 50 percent of the murders, about 38 percent of the assaults, 25 percent of the rapes, more than 70 percent of the robberies, and close to 40 percent of the kidnappings in America. There's no category of crime where blacks are underrepresented, though they are about at par when it comes to pornography offenses.[6]

These numbers aren't inflated by overpolicing, either. They are based on victim reports compiled by the FBI.

Why is black crime so high? Some people say that it's a function of poverty. But that's not really adequate to explain the prevalence of violent crime in the black community. There are enormous sections of the country that are extremely poor, with widespread drug addiction, and plenty of guns—think of northwestern Pennsylvania, or West Virginia, or a lot of the Rust Belt and Appalachia generally. There's plenty of social dysfunction there, but relatively few murders, outside of the cities. Half of American counties don't see any murder in a given year, and half of all murders are concentrated in 2 percent of all counties.[7]

There is a cultural sickness afflicting many in black America, and I believe it has a lot to do with the epidemic of fatherlessness among their families. As mentioned earlier, America, believe it or not, leads the world in single-parent households. The rate is highest among blacks, but the rate is rising among whites, too. We need to do something to turn this around, and fast.

## THE MYTH OF THE WAR ON DRUGS

Another major myth around our criminal justice system is that the War on Drugs was a racist plot cooked up by President Richard Nixon after the civil rights era in order to reimpose brutal control over America's black population.

This thesis was supposedly proven in 2016, when journalist Dan Baum—the author of the renowned 1996 drug war exposé *Smoke and Mirrors*—reported that Nixon's former White House counsel John Ehrlichman admitted to him, in 1994, that the War on Drugs was, in fact, a cynical War on Blacks. According to Baum, Ehrlichman said:

> The Nixon campaign in 1968, and the Nixon White House after that, had two enemies: the antiwar left and black people. You understand what I'm saying? We knew we couldn't make it illegal to be either against the war or black, but by getting the public to associate the hippies with marijuana and blacks with heroin, and then criminalizing both heavily, we could disrupt those communities. We could arrest their leaders, raid their homes, break up their meetings, and vilify them night after night on the evening news. Did we know we were lying about the drugs? Of course we did.

Bingo! Baum thus offered proof positive, from within the innermost circles of Nixon's presidency, that there was a government conspiracy to gin up anxiety about drugs in order to destroy the black community. This quote from Ehrlichman is trotted out constantly by prison abolitionists and Defund the Police types in order to back up their thesis that America is basically a fascist police state. But this line is almost certainly false, if not an outright hoax.

The funny thing about this damning quote is that Baum didn't include it in his 1996 book, though he claims to have heard it in 1994. His book was widely reviewed, and Baum was interviewed all over the place. He became a go-to guy for critiques of the drug war. Yet he never mentioned this quote until twenty-two years had elapsed, by which time Ehrlichman was dead.

It's true that Nixon launched a War on Drugs. But what you never hear is that the Congressional Black Caucus went to the Oval Office and demanded that he declare it! In March 1971, the Caucus, including Harlem's new congressman Charles Rangel, argued with President Nixon that he had to take extreme measures to fight drugs, which were a plague on the streets of America's inner cities. Nixon's recordings of this meeting capture Rangel pleading with the president to use his "power . . . as you would if this were a national crisis, and I think we've reached that."[8]

Charlie Rangel served in Congress for almost fifty years and was the chairman of the House Select Committee on Narcotics Abuse and Control. In 1991, he and archconservative William F. Buckley Jr. debated on television how best to deal with the drug scourge. Buckley argued for decriminalization; Rangel demanded life sentences for drug dealers and increased enforcement on the streets. "We should not allow people to distribute this poison without fear that they might be arrested, and put in jail," thundered Rangel. Drug dealers, he said, "should believe that they will be arrested and go to jail for the rest of their natural life."

In 1976, Rangel encouraged the NYPD to form a special squad to target street-level dealing—this is the same policing tactic that is now condemned as a hostile military occupation. He opposed methadone maintenance programs—nowadays, progressive cities set up "safe injection" sites so heroin addicts don't even have to switch to methadone. In the eighties he complained that President Reagan was soft on the drug problem. He supported the use of the military to eradicate coca and marijuana crops at the source in Latin America. He strongly backed the 1986 and 1994 crime bills—including the sentencing differential between powdered and crack cocaine that Michelle Alexander and Ibram X. Kendi identify as egregiously racist.

But Rangel wasn't a lone voice crying in the wilderness. The entire Congressional Black Caucus backed these same policies. Why? *Because these policies were popular among their voters.* Working-class and middle-class black people were the ones who had to deal with the disastrous effects of drugs in their communities. They were the ones who had to deal with gang violence that resulted in shoot-outs outside schools and in playgrounds. And they were the ones who had to go to precinct community meetings and beg for more officers to patrol troubled corners.

That's not to say that respectable voices in the black community wanted cops to go out and bust heads indiscriminately, or for police departments to hire hotheaded racists, which is what Black Lives Matter advocates insist is the case. But they did want real, proactive policing to keep their neighborhoods safe—even if that meant locking up the bad apples in the neighborhood, regardless of the fact that they were black.

Even now, in the age of Defund the Police, polls indicate that blacks are not in favor of reducing the police presence in their communities. Only 28 percent of black respondents indicated support for "defunding," which means that three out of four blacks opposed it. Yes, they may have issues with certain police practices, or want more community involvement with the local cops, or any other normal concerns that citizens always have regarding local government. But black Americans oppose "defunding the police" for the same reason everyone else does: because they don't want to be victimized by violent criminals. A tiny, idiotic minority of radicals has seized control of the conversation and perverted the voice of the mass of people.[9]

## THE MYTH OF WHO'S IN PRISON AND WHY

In New York City, where I live, the radicals who occupy public office insist that enforcing laws against fare evasion on the subways is an evil, racist policy that contributes to mass incarceration. But a look at the average number of people who were locked up for jumping the turnstile on any given day before the city basically gave up on enforcement was . . . one. Ditto for marijuana possession, before New York decriminalized it.

A narrative that follows from the myth of the drug war as a war on blacks is the idea that hundreds of thousands, if not millions of people have been and continue to be locked up on minor violations, usually relating to drug possession. Everyone's heard these stories—a teenager was caught smoking a joint or carrying a little bag of something, and before anyone knew what was happening, he was sentenced to a prison term of twenty-to-life: hard time for hard guys.

It's also a common assumption that America has so many people in prison because we just go crazy with handing out life sentences. Judges are just banging their gavels and giving out decades behind bars as though they get a bonus for every convict who dies of old age in jail.

Advocates for prison abolition like to peddle the story that if we just transitioned all the small-time pot peddlers and shoplifters into alternatives to prison, and let all the nonviolent prisoners out of jail, there would only be a few hard cases left, and we could concentrate our resources on getting these guys in touch with their feelings, or get them drug treatment, and then basically we could close all the prisons.

In *The New Jim Crow*, Michelle Alexander makes the bold claim that "the system of mass incarceration is structured to reward mass drug arrests and facilitate the conviction and imprisonment of an unprecedented number of Americans, whether guilty or innocent . . . the system specifically targets people of color and then relegates them to a second-class status analogous to Jim Crow." The pro-legalization Drug Policy Alliance claims, "The United States imprisons more people than any other nation in the world—largely due to the war on drugs."

The problem is that even if we let all the nonviolent people in prison out, we wouldn't do much to reduce the nation's prison population.

Advocates like Alexander often point to the large percentage of people in federal prison for drug crimes. And it's true that about half of federal prisoners are in for drug convictions. But federal prisoners account for only about 12 percent of the nation's incarcerated population, and the nature of these crimes is generally serious. These are federal crimes, after all, and simple possession of drugs does not rise to the level of a federal case. Federal drug criminals are guilty of drug trafficking: the importation or interstate movement of hefty quantities of narcotics.[10]

Just as a side note—it's ultimately a false distinction to talk about drug offenses as "nonviolent," as opposed to "violent" crimes like murder or sexual assault. Anyone who deals drugs above the most trivial level is involved in a violent criminal network. Maybe some guy who grows a few marijuana plants and sells the flowers to his friends could be defined as outside the domain of organized crime. But drug dealers, from the street on up, are engaged in an illegal operation that necessarily uses force as the arbiter of disputes. If you can't call the police or sue someone when there's a dispute in an illegal business, the only recourse is the threat of violence, if not actual violence.

A lot of drug legalization proponents claim that ending the prohibition of drugs will also end gang warfare and all the violence associated with the drug trade. But this is foolish. Drug dealers don't sell cocaine, heroin, and meth because they are expert crafts-men or are keeping up a multigenerational business based on the loving preparation of crack for their clients. They aren't criminals because drugs are illegal; they sell illegal drugs because they are criminals. Their attraction to selling drugs is based on the promise of high profits. Legalizing drugs would just lead them into some other illegal venture. Criminals aren't specialists.

In state prisons, which hold most of the country's incarcerated population, less than 15 percent of the inmates are in for drugs as their "most serious offense," and less than 4 percent are in for drug possession. Fifty-five percent of the people in prison were con-victed of violent crimes, 18 percent for property crimes, and 12 percent for "public order" violations, including weapons charges, DUI, etc.[11]

Keep in mind, too, that these are the "top charges" for which these felons have been convicted. Most people who go to prison have pled guilty to lesser charges in order to avoid stiffer sentences. So the fact that someone is in prison for a "nonviolent" drug crime is no guarantee that they are nonviolent in real life.

It's commonly said that over-sentencing has driven mass incar-ceration, with judges handing out multi-decade prison terms for first offenses. But, in fact, the majority of state-level felony convic-tions, around 60 percent, involve no prison time at all, and most people convicted of a violent felony already have a prior conviction record.

A 2018 study by the Department of Justice revealed that, con-trary to what we hear from BLM and other abolitionists, most first-time trips to prison aren't extraordinarily long. The median time spent in prison by a violent offender prior to his first release is only 2.4 years. Twenty percent of convicted murderers in prison for the first time get out in less than five years, as do almost 60 percent of rapists.

## THE REAL THUGS

No belief on the Left is more widely held than the notion that black people are routinely murdered by the police. The entire history of America for many people is understood through the idea that cops kill unarmed blacks as a matter of course—and almost always get away with it. Leftists and abolitionists are obsessed with the idea that American society invented policing as a means to monitor blacks and capture escaped slaves.

To get a sense of how stupid this narrative is, and how broadly it is repeated, consider the following "History Explained" text from the legendary and highly respected NAACP:

> The origins of modern-day policing can be traced back to the "Slave Patrol." The earliest formal slave patrol was created in the Carolinas in the early 1700s with one mission: to establish a system of terror and squash slave uprisings with the capacity to pursue, apprehend, and return runaway slaves to their owners. Tactics included the use of excessive force to control and produce desired slave behavior. . . .
>
> By the 1900s, local municipalities began to establish police departments to enforce local laws in the East and Midwest, including Jim Crow laws. Local municipalities leaned on police to enforce and exert excessive brutality on African Americans who violated any Jim Crow law. Jim Crow laws continued through the end of the 1960s.

Cities in the East and Midwest "began to establish police departments" *by the 1900s?* Doesn't the NAACP have any historians, or even vaguely literate people, on staff? All the major cities of America had official police departments, in the modern sense that we know them today, *before* the Civil War. But well before that, dating back to the earliest colonial days, America always had organized watchmen, sheriffs, and constables to catch thieves and keep the peace. This tradition goes back to England and has its origins in Anglo-Saxon common law.

The first professional municipal police force was established in London in 1829, based at Scotland Yard. Robert Peel, known as the father of modern policing, put forward his famous "General Instructions," which were issued to every new officer. The concluding point of general instruction reads, "To recognise always that the test of police efficiency is the absence of crime and disorder, and not the visible evidence of police action in dealing with them." This sentiment was adopted—perhaps imperfectly, but certainly as an ideal—by police forces around the world, including in the United States.

This crazy idea that American law enforcement is literally just a white supremacist outgrowth of the slave system is totally made-up. It's like comic book history, but unfortunately it's now spouted by people who ought to know better and is being taught to our schoolchildren.

Shortly after George Floyd's death in 2020, the House Judiciary Committee convened a special hearing on "Policing Practices and Law Enforcement Accountability." Congressman Hakeem Jeffries from Brooklyn, who is often spoken of as Nancy Pelosi's likely successor as leader of the Democrats in the House, spoke to the "innocent, unarmed African Americans [who] are repeatedly killed in policing encounter after police encounter."

This theme was repeated throughout the hearing. Vanita Gupta, head of the powerful Civil Rights Division of the Department of Justice under Obama, and associate attorney general under Biden, was a star witness for the Democrats. Referring to the George Floyd case, Gupta dismissed the idea that "the outpouring of pain and anger is anything but a reaction to one isolated incident, or the misconduct of a few bad apples." Rather, she explained, "the outcry is

a response to the long cycle of stolen lives and violence with impunity toward black people in our nation."

Gupta went on to make the same case that Defund the Police
advocates make, insisting,

We are now at a turning point. There is no returning to normal. We
have to create a new way forward, one that does more than tinker
at the edges, that promotes data and training. We need something
that truly transforms policing, and leads to more accountability for
communities. It is imperative that we get this right, and that Congress' response in this moment appropriately reflects and acknowledges the important work of Black Lives Matter, the movement for
black lives, and so many people that are bringing us to this tipping
point. . . .

[P]olicing reform alone is not going to solve the crisis that we're
in today. This moment of reckoning requires leaders, together
with communities, to envision a new paradigm of public safety
that respects the human rights of all people. That means not just
changing policing practices and culture, but ultimately shrinking the footprint of the criminal legal system in black and brown
people's lives. And it means shifting our approach to public safety
from exclusively focusing on criminalization, and policing towards
investments in economic opportunity, education, healthcare, and
other public benefits.

Make no mistake: "shrinking the footprint of the criminal legal
system" is the same thing that the most radical police abolitionists
demand. On the question of policing there is no space between
Gupta—one of Biden's top appointees, who believes that police
behave with violent impunity toward black people—and the most
radical bomb-throwing street rioter. It's just a question of tactics.

When Biden says, as he did in May 2022, that he wants to

"Fund the police! Fund the police!" remember that Gupta is in the number three spot at the Department of Justice, and he put her there.[12]

This view is commonly held. Nusrat Choudhury was nominated by President Biden for a federal judgeship. At her confirmation hearing, it was noted by Senator John N. Kennedy of Louisiana that in 2015 she said, on a panel at Princeton University, that "the killing of unarmed black men by police happens every day in America." Asked if she believes that statistic to be valid, she excused herself by saying she was "engaging in rhetorical advocacy."

Sorry, but "engaging in rhetorical advocacy" sounds like a fancy way of saying "I'm lying."

So, we have all heard the Left talk about the rows of black corpses that the police are constantly leaving on the streets of America. But we don't really hear too much about what the real numbers are. Let's get down to brass tacks.

Nobody keeps detailed statistics. But to its credit, the *Washington Post* assembled a database on police shootings that people on both sides agree is roughly accurate. They found that, in an average year, police shoot and kill about 1,000 people—black, white, Hispanic, Asian. That's 1,000 for the whole year, or fewer than three per day.

That doesn't sound too fantastic, to be frank. However, that number includes people who are armed and dangerous, shooting at the police or attacking members of the public. People who brandish knives, or use a car as a weapon. When you get down to the number of unarmed people who are killed by the police, the pool is winnowed down substantially.

According to the *Post*, 7,330 people were shot and killed by the police between 2015 and the first few months of 2022. Of these, 58 percent had a gun. There were 445 *unarmed* people shot and killed by the cops in those seven years, about 30 percent of whom were black.[13]

Do you see where we are headed? The number of unarmed black people who are shot and killed by the police every year is in the low two digits, and is substantially less than the number of white people killed in similar circumstances. Yes, of course there are more white people in America, and the rate of black people killed by the police is higher than the rate for white people. But the fact of crime and criminality in America is that it's highly concentrated in black neighborhoods, so black people wind up having more police interactions than white people do.

Roland Fryer Jr. is considered one of the top economists in the country. At thirty, he became the youngest black person to get tenure at Harvard. Fryer won a MacArthur "genius" grant for his groundbreaking work demonstrating that the black-white achievement gap among grade schoolers could be narrowed when accounting for socioeconomic factors, including parent involvement in reading with their children.

Fryer turned his prodigious brainpower to the question of police shootings in order to determine exactly how badly blacks fared in confrontations with law enforcement. His findings rocked academia and the charitable foundation world. Police did have a higher rate of use of nonlethal force when arresting black suspects, but when it came to shootings, he found "no racial differences in either the raw data or when contextual factors are taken into account."

It's no real surprise why this is the case. Can you name any white person who was killed by the police in the last five or ten years? Probably not, but I bet you could rattle off half-a-dozen names of blacks who were killed, even though there are many more whites killed by law enforcement. But cops killing white people doesn't gain any traction in the media, because it doesn't promote or contribute to the anti-police narrative. Black lives only matter when a black life is taken by a white cop. That way they can promote their agenda of seizing more power and influence.

Justine Damond, a white woman, was shot and killed by a Minneapolis police officer (who happened to be black) after she called the police in July 2017 because she thought she heard a woman in distress. She was sitting in her car when Officer Mohamed Noor shot her for apparently no reason. He was tried and went to jail for a few years. No riots broke out, nor did Minneapolis burn. But when a police officer kills a black person, there is a solid chance that their life and career will be thrust into the national spotlight, they will be accused of racial hatred, and they may even face criminal charges.

As a result, cops are much more careful about shooting black suspects—perhaps to the detriment of their own safety. Killing of cops soared in 2021, reaching a historic high of seventy-two officers murdered on the job. It's perhaps worth noting that black offenders tend to be responsible in about one-third of these cases. Blacks, that is to say, kill cops at about the same rate of disproportionality to their numbers as they are killed by them.

An intriguing poll was conducted asking people to identify their political leaning, and then to estimate how many unarmed black men were murdered by the police in 2019. Half of the "very liberal" respondents believed 1,000 or more unarmed black men were killed by the cops in that one year. About 25 percent believed the number to be 10,000 or more![14]

Depending on which database you consult, between 12 and 27 unarmed black men were killed by the police in 2019. This is one of the reasons why BLM advocates are always screaming the names of their martyrs and demanding that we "Say Their Names!" The statistics for their arguments are pretty unimpressive, so it's much more effective for them to make it personal.

We have a major problem here, because a large segment of the electorate has been fed a pack of lies about police violence that does not reflect reality. If our country is ever to come to its senses, we need to overcome the Left's reliance on a cheap narrative of race and blood guilt that simply doesn't add up.

# CHAPTER SIX

## When Prosecutors Prefer Criminals

AMERICA'S GREATNESS COMES FROM our long tradition of individual liberty. Everyone is born equally free and is allowed to pursue his own destiny, reaping the rewards of their labor, talent, and luck—or taking their knocks when they deserve them. But the American system demands a strong rule of law, which means an effective court system.

Our system of justice is not perfect, of course, but it affords and guarantees protection for people accused of crimes. Even the most heinous criminals, about whom there is no doubt of their guilt, are ensured "due process." The state must argue its case in front of an independent judge and a jury of his peers. The defendant may examine the state's evidence, question witnesses, and present his own arguments. He must be allowed to have an attorney, and his silence may not be taken as evidence of guilt.

These safeguards are precious. I wouldn't want to live in a society where individuals accused of serious offenses lacked even the slightest of these rights, and I don't imagine you would, either. The power of the state, compared to that of even a wealthy and powerful individual, is awesome. Without the protections outlined in the Bill of Rights, we would be crushed by the whims of a fickle government that could pursue us for political, personal, or pecuniary reasons.

At the same time, though, "the state"—which in a political philosophy seminar may be presented as a totalizing force with unlimited money and power—is typically understaffed and faces demands that far outstrip its actual resources. In a system governed by the rule of law, crime victims are not allowed to seek justice through revenge or vendetta or by the payment of blood money. People who are victimized by others rely on the state to impose justice on their behalf.

If you are, for instance, beaten up by a street thug, your suffering and the damage to your person and livelihood are borne by you and your loved ones. Your pain is yours alone and the loneliness of victimization is acute. You have to pay your own hospital bills, and your loved ones, if you die, will have to pay for your funeral. If you miss work or lose your job, you will have to figure out a new way to make a living, or maybe go on public assistance.

Whenever I hear about a mass shooting—the sort where maybe no one is killed but some are "only wounded"—I always think about what happens to the wounded. Having seen combat, I have met my share of fellow Marines and other servicemen and -women who were wounded. It's not like the movies, where you get patched up and are good to go. People who are shot can lose limbs. They can suffer major internal damage that never really heals correctly. They may walk with limps or prosthetics forever.

If you are run over by a car driven by someone with insurance, or suffer medical malpractice, or a tree limb breaks in a city park and injures you, our legal system of torts provides for the assign-ment of blame and just compensation. People who get maimed in these circumstances can receive hefty seven- or eight-figure settle-ments to account for their pain, suffering, and loss of income.

But if some maniac shoves you in front of a subway train and you lose your legs, or a mugger knocks you over the head and leaves you with brain damage and blinding headaches for the rest of your life, you are basically out of luck. You can sue your attacker, but they often don't have enough assets to cover the cost of postage to mail back their summons.

In these situations, the criminal justice system may be your only ally, and offer the only opportunity to achieve a sense of fair-ness and closure. The court system may not be able to restore your health or your property, but knowing that someone who has caused you injury is being held to account for his actions is some-thing that crime victims and their families live for. It literally keeps them going.

## THE LAW PROTECTS THE LITTLE GUY

So the government, which conservatives often scrutinize with a healthy dose of mistrust, is actually the best friend the little guy has when it comes to rectifying criminal wrongs. This is the sense in which the government in criminal trials calls itself "The People." But think of that hoary phrase in lowercase, as in "the people" who get hurt by violent criminals who have no regard for public order or the sanctity of the individual. That's who looks to the court system to remedy the pain and loss they have suffered and for which there is no other compensation on the planet.

Cops are the first line of defense in public safety. But without a functioning court system to mete out justice, there can be no real law and order. That's why honest courts are so essential to civilization, and why prosecutors play such a vital function in society. Prosecutors—the government lawyers who pursue criminal charges against wrongdoers—are the ones who ensure that bad guys face consequences.

We rely on prosecutors to be meticulously careful in assembling their case against a defendant suspected of criminality. Under our system of rights, it is the job of the state to convince the jury that the suspect is guilty; he doesn't have to say a thing. The burden is entirely on the prosecutor to establish guilt, and he has to tread carefully, because any mistake in collecting or presenting solid evidence can lead to its exclusion from trial, meaning that the guilty may walk free. Solid prosecution in the service of safe communities requires zealous advocacy in the pursuit of justice, meticulous preparation, and an abiding sense of care and concern for the victims of crime.

This is why prosecutors have traditionally been law-and-order types first and foremost—typically on the conservative side, even when they are Democrats, as most big-city district attorneys usually are. People who decide to become prosecutors—district attorneys or states attorneys at the local level, or attorneys general at the state level—have an inclination toward pursuing justice through the just punishment of crime. The people who are more worried about the rights of the accused have generally gravitated toward becoming public defenders. It's a division of labor that has made sense.

Lead prosecutors hold an elected position, whereas public defenders are usually either appointed or hold jobs within the civil service, though there are jurisdictions, including Florida and San Francisco, where the public defender is elected. But it says a lot about the role of the prosecutor as an advocate for "The People" that the office is filled by the candidate who most vigorously promises to pursue justice for the victims of crime—not for the producers of it.

For as long as anyone can remember, that's how it worked. Whether they ran as Republicans or Democrats, prosecutors have had an orientation that was geared toward locking up criminals. Some may have promised to focus more on organized crime, others on street crime; some may have wanted to take on public corruption, while others swore to target white-collar crime. Many prosecutors were effective, and many were ineffective. Many were showboaters who wanted to get in the papers more than anything else, and others were lazy or even corrupt. But they all generally stood for the same thing: protecting the law-abiding citizenry from the criminal element.

Starting less than a decade ago, radicals seeking to subvert and destroy the American system of criminal justice—which they believed to be savagely racist, unfair, and essentially an outgrowth and continuation of the Jim Crow system of discrimination—realized that prosecutors' offices were a weak link in the chain of law and order. Elections for district attorney are low-cost campaigns that don't usually attract a lot of attention. Targeting these races with even moderate resources could deliver outsize payoffs by replacing traditional prosecutors with hard-core leftist abolitionists, typically from the defense side of the equation, who would pledge to eliminate what they characterized as institutionalized racial biases in charging and sentences.

The results have been extraordinarily successful—for the proponents of disorder. Across the nation, this new breed of progressive prosecutors has run in and won dozens of local elections by campaigning on a platform of lies about racial inequities, police brutality, and mass incarceration. Adopting a message of "Safety and Justice," these radicals have insisted that "you can't arrest your way to safety," and that "addressing the root social causes" of crime is the best way to reduce it. By refusing to prosecute perps for many "minor" crimes, seeking "alternatives to incarceration" for people convicted of even serious crimes, and freeing felons from prison early, these progressive prosecutors have contributed to the escalation of crime in and the destruction of American cities.

It's perhaps unfair to blame a prosecutor for a large city's violent crime. Surely there are myriad causes underlying such widespread bloodshed and dysfunction. But the local prosecutor has enormous influence over the culture and tone of criminality, and sets the parameters of what criminals feel they can get away with.

A law-abiding person has a mindset that is completely different from that of a habitual criminal. For instance, when you walk into a store, do you quickly scan the ceilings for where the cameras and mirrors are? Do you size up the security personnel and make a snap judgment about how willing they would be to chase you, and if they did, how easily you could beat them up? When you walk down the street, are you acutely aware of the presence of police? Do you look at people approaching you and take a quick guess about how much money they are carrying?

Probably not, because you aren't always thinking about how to steal something or rob someone. But the criminal perspective is predatory—or parasitical—and essentially opportunistic. Progressives like to contend that crime is driven not by individual choice but by economic necessity born of social inequality, and as such, policing is ineffective because street crime is a matter of urgent need. But habitual criminals are acutely attuned to the climate of enforcement and are extremely sensitive to the nuances of heightened security.

Anyone who has dealt with groups of children—a first-grade teacher, say—understands the dynamic. Some kids will always test the limits of what is considered unacceptable, and try to push the envelope of impunity, often to the point where keeping an orderly classroom or playground is impossible.

Real criminals—or the grown-up versions of the junior variety—

are the same way. If they notice that the cops no longer tell them to stop drinking beer on the stoop, maybe they will take a six-pack to the park and drink it there. If nobody stops them from blasting music on the sidewalk, maybe they will start a dice game to see what happens. If selling marijuana no longer draws charges, why not upgrade to selling a higher-margin product like crack?

Prosecutors determine what happens after cops arrest someone. They decide whether to charge a perp with a felony or misdemeanor. They decide whether to ask for bail or let someone go free to await trial at home. They ask judges to send the guilty to jail or let them off with probation. Prosecutors set the whole tone of enforcement, and the police follow their lead. If prosecutors indicate that they aren't going to pursue charges against shoplifters, then the cops will stop arresting them. And if criminals know they aren't going to face serious consequences, they will commit more crime.

Progressives live in a fantasy world where enforcement is the cause of crime, but here on earth we know that if you let people get away with stuff, you will get more of it.

## RUINING CITIES

San Francisco is a jewel among America's cities. Famous for more than a century for its bohemian vibe, San Francisco was responsible for the birth of hippie culture, gay liberation, and the tech revolution—whether you appreciate its cultural influence or not, there's no denying the fact that the city punches above its weight. Its dramatic streetscape, waterfront, and picturesque Victorian housing stock have made it a must for tourists and formed the backdrop of many classic movies and TV shows.

In recent years, though, San Francisco's tolerant attitude toward its streets—which has usually included a permissive approach to nudity, drugs, and homelessness—has spilled over into a kind of anarchy. Homeless people are permitted to set up tent encampments wherever they like, making sidewalks impassable. Once-peaceful residential districts are covered in human fecal waste, and pedestrians have to be careful not to step on discarded syringes. The city has the nation's highest rate of drug overdose deaths. Crime has spiked. It is not unusual for smash-and-grab robbers to calmly break car windows and steal whatever's in view, in the middle of the day, with no fear of arrest.

Amid this growing crisis, in 2019 the city elected as its twenty-ninth district attorney the one man raised practically from birth to make things worse. Chesa Boudin first came to public attention as a baby, when his parents dropped him off with a babysitter on their way to participate in a bank robbery, which resulted in the murder of two policemen and a security guard in Westchester County, New York, in 1981.

His parents, Kathy Boudin and David Gilbert, were core members of the notorious leftist terror group the Weather Underground Organization (originally called "Weatherman" in homage to the classic Bob Dylan tune "Subterranean Homesick Blues," which proclaimed, "You don't need a weatherman to know which way the wind blows"). The Weather Underground, which described itself as a "white fighting force" in alliance with the forces of black liberation, conducted a series of bombings in the sixties and seventies, mostly in protest of the war in Vietnam.

On March 1, 1971, the Weather Underground bombed the U.S. Capitol; a year later it bombed the Pentagon. Though the war was largely over by 1975, the organization bombed the State Department in January of that year. The group issued a communiqué explaining that "the imperialists who run this country are responsible for hunger, unemployment and racist repression against Black and Third World people. . . . The government that divides us against each other through racism, also tries to divide us from the people in the world who are liberating themselves. . . ."

Future district attorney Boudin's mom and dad didn't just bomb federal buildings during that period, though—they also set off powerful explosive devices at corporate headquarters in Pittsburgh and New York, and bombed state offices in California, too. It is true that the bombs were timed to go off at night, and no one was killed during this reign of terror, which apologists for these radicals like to point to as evidence of their benign intentions. They just wanted peace!

It's amazing to think that none of this gang went to prison for their years of bombing important monuments and buildings—including the Capitol building. Charges were dropped against the Weather Underground and other radical terror groups in the wake of Watergate, when the FBI and other intelligence groups were discredited by the findings of the congressional Church Committee. Reports that the FBI had run counterintelligence and disinformation campaigns against the radical Left scandalized sympathetic liberals, and the general climate of the Jimmy Carter years—which included a general amnesty for Vietnam War draft dodgers—contributed to a disinclination to prosecute left-wing terrorists.

Many radicals emerged from hiding during this period to receive slaps on the wrist, at most, for their criminal activity. Celebrated militants Bernardine Dohrn and Bill Ayers—a married couple who would go on to mentor Barack Obama—mainstreamed themselves, becoming tenured professors in Chicago. But some of their comrades stayed underground, still committed to the lofty ideals of violent revolution.

Kathy Boudin was a princess of the radical Left. Her great-uncle was a prominent socialist in the early 1900s and a noted Marxist theorist. Her father, Leonard Boudin, was a famous lawyer who defended many communists and other high-profile defendants. David Gilbert, her partner, grew up upper-middle-class in Brookline, Massachusetts, and founded the Columbia University chapter of Students for a Democratic Society. The duo elected to remain in the shadows during the amnesty period, as members of the far-left May 19th Communist Organization.

In the late 1970s, the couple joined the Revolutionary Armed Task Force, a white auxiliary to the Black Liberation Army. On October 20, 1981, Boudin dropped her fourteen-month-old baby, Chesa, with a babysitter and took the wheel of a rented U-Haul to help rob a Brink's truck of $1.6 million. One of the Brink's guards was killed; the other was wounded and survived, only to die in the World Trade Center attacks on 9/11. Boudin served as a getaway driver; because the stickup men were all black, having a white woman drive the truck was meant to fool the police. Upon being stopped by the cops, Kathy Boudin emerged from the U-Haul and urged the officers to holster their weapons, at which point her armed confederates leapt from the truck with guns blazing. Two of the officers—Waverly Brown (who was black) and Edward O'Grady Jr.—were killed.

At trial, David Gilbert proclaimed himself at war with the U.S. government and refused to offer a defense; he was found guilty and sentenced to seventy-five years to life. Kathy Boudin pled guilty to one count of felony murder and robbery and took a twenty-to-life sentence. She was paroled in 2003 and went on to become a professor at Columbia University and, later, a scholar-in-residence at New York University School of Law. Gilbert, who was expected to stay in prison forever, had his sentence commuted by Andrew Cuomo on Cuomo's last day in office as governor in 2021. Gilbert walked free a few months later.

I only go into all this ancient history to give a sense of Chesa Boudin's background. With his parents in jail, he was raised by their good friends Bernardine Dohrn and Bill Ayers and steeped in an ethic of radical politics, revolution, and self-pity. As a kind of tragic orphan of the social justice wars, Chesa Boudin was spiritually adopted by the American Left elite, which made sure he wanted for nothing and was put on the fast track to the big leagues. He attended Yale, and then got a Rhodes scholarship to attend Oxford. He then went to Venezuela to sit at the feet of Marxist dictator Hugo Chavez; Boudin translated Chavez's propaganda into English, and also authored, with the help of a Chavez aide, a book of questions-and-answers about the Venezuelan Revolution, aimed at American college students. Boudin then returned to Yale for law school, after which he landed highly prestigious clerkships with prominent federal judges, including Charles Breyer, brother of Supreme Court justice Stephen Breyer.

Writing about his childhood, Chesa Boudin always speaks mournfully about the injustice of his parents' separation from him, and the unfairness of their sentences. "Neither of my parents was armed or intended for anyone to get hurt," Boudin wrote in the *Nation* in 2021 as part of a major PR push to get his father released. "My parents were arrested and charged with felony murder—an anachronistic legal doctrine that allows prosecutors to punish almost any participant in a serious crime resulting in death, no matter their role, with murder."

Sure, if his parents' involvement with the Brink's robbery had been limited to making sandwiches for the gunmen, maybe a felony murder conviction would have been excessive. But they were there and engaged the whole time. His mother tricked the police into putting their weapons down, and his dad was part of another getaway crew.

Chesa Boudin refuses to this day to admit that his parents were terroristic criminals. Instead he sees them—and himself—as the victims of "our country's retributive obsession with prisons." He recalls "waiting in lines to get through metal detectors, steel gates, and pat searches just to see my parents, just to give them a hug." He explains that his "parents' crime had been organized by the Black Liberation Army, and that they were in it not for money but because of a misguided vision of radical racial solidarity."

If these were the words of a poet or a sociology professor it would pass without comment, because it's no surprise that the children of imprisoned terrorists would side with their parents and retain a sense of bitterness into adulthood. But Chesa Boudin became the lead prosecutor of a major American city that has famously fallen into major dysfunction. What the hell is going on in this country that someone like Chesa Boudin—an out-and-out communist sympathizer and apologist for racial terror—is the district attorney of San Francisco?

Boudin ran for office never having prosecuted a case. His entire professional legal experience before becoming district attorney was as a San Francisco public defender, in which role he advocated for the abolition of bail. In 2017 Boudin characterized the entire San Francisco Police Department as "rogue," saying that "the statistics show that police go for their guns, and that's a big problem, and it's a problem that results in the loss of life." In 2016, the previous year, San Francisco police officers shot four people, killing three, all of whom were armed. That same year there were more than sixty thousand "reported incidents" to the SFPD, so it was grossly unfair to accuse the cops of routinely shooting people in the course of their duties.

Chesa Boudin's 2019 campaign for district attorney was based on his success in disrupting California's bail laws with a high-profile lawsuit that remains tied up in the courts, and by promising to "do something other than just double down on harsher convictions and longer sentences." Saying that "the system is broken," Boudin stressed his "creativity" and "insight," promising "equal treatment, an end to mass incarceration, and redemption and rehabilitation instead of recidivism." These are the kinds of sunny words we have become used to hearing from progressive criminal justice reformers across the country. But when it comes to specifics, things get fuzzy fast.

Boudin cited dubious statistics, claiming "that more than 50 percent of Americans have an immediate family member either currently or formerly incarcerated," which "tells you a lot about just how defining a feature of American culture incarceration has become." This is the kind of misleading data that hard-core leftist prison abolitionists like Chesa Boudin spout all the time. The survey in question asked respondents if anyone in their family they felt "close" to had ever spent a night in jail and found that about 45 percent answered affirmatively.

But since this figure includes not just parents, children, siblings, and intimate partners, but also an expanded definition of "family" that can count grandparents and grandchildren, in-laws, and cousins, too, it's easy to see how the concept of "family incarceration" can easily generate inflated numbers in order to push a narrative of intense intergenerational disruption caused by a "culture of incarceration." But in all honesty, how deeply does it really impact an extended family of eight or ten individuals if one bad apple spent a night in jail once or twice?

Boudin ran for office at a moment when violent crime was relatively low in San Francisco, though property crime—especially auto theft and "smash-and-grabs"—were up. He laughed off these concerns, saying, "We're lucky in San Francisco that we're in a position where the thing people are talking about is auto burglaries."

This scorn is typical of the liberal mindset, which sees property crime as essentially victimless and certainly not worth prosecuting. Boudin, like other progressive prosecutors around the country, sniffs at pursuing minor crime, which he sees as a waste of resources. But minor crime for someone like Boudin is any crime that isn't happening to him.

After Boudin took office, things in San Francisco went from bad to much, much worse. Murders spiked in 2020 and 2021, and felony assaults—including anti-Asian hate-based assaults—were up, too. But arrests dropped by about a third, as the district attorney signaled he wouldn't bother prosecuting many cases. In 2019, the prosecutor's office achieved convictions in 60 percent of cases that went to trial; by 2022 that figure had fallen to 34 percent, with more defendants getting "diverted" to non-jail alternatives. Even as crime soared in 2021, people convicted in San Francisco of felony charges had a better-than-even chance of being sentenced to probation.

The results have been a disaster. Viral videos have depicted thieves moseying around CVS and filling large garbage bags with whatever they can sell for dope money; seventeen drugstores have closed their doors for good. Fatal drug overdoses have doubled. Murder is up. The year 2021 saw a 567 percent increase in hate crimes against Asians. Union Square—the city's tony shopping district—was assailed by masked looters who would storm high-end retailers like Louis Vuitton and Bloomingdale's, running out with armloads of designer purses.

Chesa Boudin is a particularly interesting case of a modern progressive prosecutor, and the rapid decline of San Francisco—a fantastically wealthy and beautiful city—is a remarkable illustration of how failed policies can destroy public order. Sickened by the decay and chaos, San Francisco recalled Boudin in June 2022, preventing him from poisoning the city with his wicked ideology any longer. But Boudin's type is common as dirt. Across the country, prosecutors espousing the same empty principles of more justice for criminals and less safety for everyone else have been busy destroying American cities that fought like hell to overcome the despair and misery of the 1990s.

## SECOND TO NONE

In Chicago, Kim Foxx took over the office of the Cook County state's attorney in late 2016, elected on a platform of reform. She made the familiar liberal pledges of diversion of "low-level offenders" to treatment, a crackdown on police brutality, and an end to mass incarceration. But ever since she took charge of prosecuting crime in the City of Big Shoulders, Chicago has become a national embarrassment.

Weekends with thirty or fifty shooting victims have become routine in Chicago, or "Chiraq," as embittered locals call it. In 2020, carjackings more than doubled over the previous year, with some months seeing five or six "vehicular hijackings" per day. Murders increased by 55 percent from 2019 to 2020 (while total arrests fell by 42 percent) and rose again in 2021, making it the bloodiest year in a quarter century.

Is all this Kim Foxx's fault? Maybe not all of it, but she has done her part. In the midafternoon of August 15, 2021, two little girls, Serenity and Aubrey Broughton, were getting into the family car after visiting their grandmother in the Belmont neighborhood of northwest Chicago. Their mother and father had just buckled the girls, aged seven and six, into their car seats when a car pulled up, and three men got out and started shooting in their direction. They fired twenty-nine shots. Aubrey was shot in the chest and her lung was punctured; her sister was shot in the chest and torso and died.

Police worked feverishly to identify a suspect, but Foxx's office declined to prosecute him on the grounds that the evidence was insufficient. Convinced their case was solid, the cops went directly to a judge—an unusual but legitimate move—who ordered Aireon Luster held and charged with murder. Chagrined that the police had essentially gone around her office, Foxx called top brass to have Luster "uncharged" and set free. The resulting turmoil deeply soured relations between Chicago PD and the state's attorney's office, with insults and imprecations flowing freely between them. Finally, after a public outcry threatened to embarrass Foxx's office, Luster was re-arrested, charged, and held without bail. Luster has pled not guilty and has not yet been convicted. But the cops learned that the city's top prosecutor mistrusts them and doesn't have their back, and she doesn't have the backs of the city's kids, either.

Around that same time, police arrested five gang members after a wild midmorning shoot-out in the Austin neighborhood that killed one, and left two of the suspects wounded. Chicago police sought to charge all five of the gangbangers with murder, but Foxx refused to file charges, and the thugs were all released without charges. How come? Foxx determined that the shoot-out was "mutual combat," an archaic legal term that usually applies to bar fights or other scuffles where an evenly matched pair agree to fight each other, and nobody else is hurt or threatened. It was never meant to describe multiple armed gunmen shooting at each other in a crowded neighborhood.

Foxx's most famous refusal to prosecute, of course, was in the 2019 case of Jussie Smollett, the TV actor and well-connected Democrat who staged a bizarre and farcical hate crime against himself with the help of two Nigerian brothers who stood in for racist, homophobic Trump supporters. Smollett's alleged victimization summoned outrage from Hollywood types, who couldn't get enough of weeping over the violence and hatred that Trump inspired. Chicago police put in weeks of overtime looking to snag the MAGA creeps who had attacked Smollett before concluding that the whole thing was a hoax.

It looked pretty bad for Smollett, but then Foxx's office, apparently with the urging of Michelle Obama's chief of staff, Tina Tchen (who seems to have intervened as a family friend), dropped all charges against him and sealed the record of the case. Foxx had recused herself from the prosecution after it emerged that she had been in close communication with Smollett's family, giving them assurances that everything would turn out well for him.

A special prosecutor was appointed to the case, and ultimately Smollett was found guilty of five felony counts of lying to the police. He never confessed to the hoax and continues to maintain his innocence. Nobody believes him. He is widely acknowledged to be a liar and a demented narcissist. But after he was sentenced to jail, Foxx went out of her way to defend him in an op-ed, saying that the prosecution of Smollett was a "kangaroo" trial and an example of "mob justice."

But most tellingly, Foxx claimed that the special prosecution against Smollett was really targeting her and her fellow progressive prosecutors around the country. It "sets a precedent," Foxx wrote, "that can be weaponized against progressive prosecutors determined to break the cycle of inevitable outcomes. Further, I worry it will serve as a deterrent to the next generation of prosecutors eager to fight for critical reforms. Anyone interested in an equitable system of justice should be worried too."

In other words, an attack on her bad policies is an attack on justice itself. This is a common response among the progressive Left, and excuses a wide range of sins.

## BIG ROTTEN APPLE

New York City has five district attorneys—one for each borough—and progressives have steadily taken over the city. As discussed already, New York saw a miraculous turnaround in fortunes after the introduction of proactive policing in the early 1990s. Homicides dropped from over 2,000 in 1991 to less than 300 a quarter century later. But a massive reengineering of the criminal justice system, and a shift in focus toward helping criminals instead of jailing them, led to a stunning collapse in public order.

The election of Alvin Bragg to the storied seat of Manhattan district attorney—once held by the legendary Thomas Dewey—alarmed New Yorkers, who awoke after his inauguration to find, that they had installed a radical activist who embraced a "presumption of non-incarceration." Elected in a low-turnout primary, Bragg benefited from a rigged system that aims to keep people uninterested in elections. Except in cases of rape, murder, or armed assault that results in serious injury, Bragg explained, "non-incarceration is the outcome for every case." In other words, virtually nobody should go to jail.

Bragg promised to end punishment and expand "restorative justice," which focuses on the "core drivers of violence." Restorative justice, he explains, "focuses on harm to the victim but also the needs of victims, communities, and offenders, and addresses obligations that result from those harms through the use of inclusive, collaborative processes by those with a stake in the outcome." It "encourages accountability, creates safety, reduces the prison population, individualizes the approach to meet the needs of those involved, and works toward healing trauma or harm."

Bragg compares the "serious breakdown of trust between communities of color and law enforcement in New York City" to the brutality of apartheid South Africa, and explains that "just as Truth and Reconciliation Commissions can be useful in repairing harm when a government has perpetrated harm on their own communities," so too can restorative justice repair the harms that the NYPD and the court system have inflicted on "communities of color" in New York.

Doesn't that sound great? Unfortunately, once you dig beyond all the fine-sounding words to figure out what restorative justice does, rather than just how its supporters like to talk about its effects, you find . . . more words. It appears that "restorative justice solutions" amount to bullying crime victims into listening to their assailants tell sad stories about their lives, and then allow them to apologize to each other for the mutual harms they have suffered.

It's worth noting that in the first few months of Bragg's term, serious crime in Manhattan rose about 60 percent versus the year before—which had already seen a sharp rise in crime.

I could easily write this whole book about progressive prosecutors and the insane damage they are doing across the nation. From Marilyn Mosby in Baltimore to Larry Krasner in Philadelphia, from Eric Gonzalez in Brooklyn to George Gascón in Los Angeles, radical abolitionists have seized control of the levers of prosecution and thrust the gears of public safety into reverse.

## BAD BILLIONAIRE

I won't belabor the point. But it is worth ending this chapter by pointing to the one individual who has done more to advance this destruction campaign across America than anyone else. George Soros is a stupendously wealthy investor who has dedicated vast sums to progressive causes via his Open Society Foundations, which has a $20 billion endowment. The Open Society has poured hundreds of millions of dollars into Black Lives Matter and other organizations that have sponsored civil unrest following the deaths of Michael Brown, Trayvon Martin, and George Floyd. The OSF has been a major proponent of drug legalization for decades, supports open borders, and promotes boycotting of Israel.

Soros has, both personally and through various funding entities, heavily supported Democratic candidates, including Barack Obama, Hillary Clinton, and Joe Biden. He helped create the Democratic powerhouse advocacy group the Center for American Progress (CAP), which effectively operates as a tax-exempt arm of the Democratic National Committee. After the election of Trump in 2016, CAP, armed with Soros money, pledged to become the "nerve center for the anti–Donald Trump resistance." CAP is now headed by Patrick Gaspard, a former Obama appointee and the former president of the Open Society Foundations.

Soros has given many millions of dollars to local district attorney candidates who align themselves with his agenda for the American criminal justice system. So it is important to look at Soros and his activities as a whole, and to understand what's happening in our cities as integral to the Democratic vision for the country. The imposition of a radical agenda inside our district attorney offices does not run counter to mainstream Democratic politics, no matter how many times Joe Biden squawks, "Fund the police! Fund the police!" Soros is funding riots in Minneapolis, the election of "centrist" Democrat leaders, the wholesale dismantling of the frame of public safety, and even the candidacy of poachers-turned-gamekeepers in our prosecutors. Not to blame everything on one man, but he accurately represents the nexus of power and money that is, bizarrely, directed toward destroying our nation.

# CHAPTER SEVEN

## Nations Are Their Borders

WHEN DONALD TRUMP ANNOUNCED in 2015 that he planned to build a wall on the Mexican border in order to keep illegal aliens out of the country, he spoke for many Americans who were frustrated that their leaders had dithered, for decades, about doing anything to stop a major problem.

Our borders are porous. Millions of people—who knows how many—are here in the country illegally, and hundreds of thousands more are permitted to enter every year. There are laws on the books about arresting and deporting them, and forbidding them from taking jobs, but these laws are scarcely enforced. Illegal aliens crowd our "sanctuary cities," use public resources, commit crime, and claim benefits. Politicians on both sides of the aisle have implicitly conspired to let it happen: Democrats who thought they were getting future voters, and Republicans who thought they were getting cheap labor. Americans, meanwhile, got the shaft.

The issue of illegal immigration has polled high as a matter of major concern for years, but it's basically been a "third rail" of politics. Nobody wanted to touch it. Trump, with his genius for tapping popular sentiment, laid the facts on the table during his initial run for presidency. "You either have a border, or you don't have a border," he told a New Hampshire crowd in December 2015. "And if you don't have a border, you don't have a country."

As a means of differentiating himself from the crowded field that year, the focus on illegal immigration was dynamite. Republican voters were beside themselves at the way Trump cut through the rhetoric, nostalgia, and sentiment to get at the heart of the matter. Immigration, he emphasized, is a good thing for America. But why can't it be orderly and rational? Countries like Canada and Australia have a lot of immigration, but they are choosy about who gets in. Why can't America act the same way?

When I was a kid on Long Island, I would read tales of adventure wherein young men could head out west or go to sea, go "off the grid," and adopt a new identity. This always sounded great. I knew from my dad that these fantasies were impossible, because modern databases and information technology mean that there's no escaping ourselves. There's no Wild West to disappear in anymore.

Unless, of course, you come from somewhere else. In that case, it's easy to come to the U.S. and disappear. Say you are a Mexican drug dealer and you get in hot water with your gang, or the government wants to arrest you. Maybe you are tired of your wife and children and want a fresh start—to pursue the proverbial "better life" for yourself in America.

If you cross the border into the United States, you can immediately head to one of our many sanctuary jurisdictions, where by law or executive order the police and local government refuse to cooperate with federal immigration authorities. You can make up a name and get a job working under the table for cash, which saves you payroll taxes. Or for a few bucks you can buy a stolen Social Security number to get a regular job, assuming your employer bothers to follow the law.

Who's going to know? Your fingerprints aren't on file in the federal N-DEx system, the National Crime Information Center (NCIC), the Interstate Identification Index (III), or the Next Generation Identification (NGI) systems, which contain records on tens of millions of Americans. And if you are careful not to get arrested for a serious crime, nobody will ever be the wiser.

When Trump asked why we were letting people come live here without vetting them or knowing anything about them, he probably didn't understand that he was shaking a box of bees. Borders and immigration are a very touchy subject. In his famous "escalator" speech, Trump said that "when Mexico sends its people, they're not sending their best. They're sending people that have lots of problems, and they're bringing those problems to us. They're bringing drugs. They're bringing crime. They're rapists."

I was in the room when Trump gave that incredible speech, and I didn't think anything of that comment. It certainly didn't come across the way it's been characterized. Writer Salena Zito said of Trump that his detractors take him literally, but not seriously, while his supporters take him seriously, but not literally. New Yorkers are brash and we talk with a certain degree of hyperbole. Everyone who heard Trump that day knew what he meant. Obviously, he wasn't saying that all Mexicans are criminals and rapists, though it's undeniable that some are. But it happens to be true and a matter of common sense that the sort of people who sneak over borders illegally are probably not the same ones we would choose to bring over, if it were up to us.

But it's not up to us. The problem with our current system is not that every illegal immigrant is a bad person or a criminal or a rapist. The problem is that we don't know—and moreover, we are *not allowed* to know—who they are at all. The people in charge have set it up so that it is literally not America's business who gets to come here. And that's a recipe for total disaster. Trump was right: a nation without a border is no nation at all.

There are libertarians and other idealists (or cynics) on the Right who believe that America should open its borders and permit anyone to come here who wants to, but they couple this proposal with the elimination of most taxes and nearly all welfare programs. This is not a realistic program and doesn't capture a lot of serious attention. There's not much chance that we are going to turn America into a capitalist free-for-all with no social safety net, where people come to hang their hat and make a buck. We are a nation, with values and history. That's important and worth preserving.

What seems a lot more likely to happen to America is some accelerated version of what we have already going on: borders that are just difficult enough to cross to keep out the disabled or elderly while permitting anyone who is strong enough to walk across miles of desert to get in. It's like a savage competition out of a dystopian novel: if you get through the horrible obstacle course, you win the prize and can work illegally in a meatpacking plant or as a grounds-keeper. You can have American babies who will anchor your presence here. In many places, including New York, you can have free access to high-quality health care.

## WRETCHED REFUSE

We hear all the time that "America is a nation of immigrants," and therefore nobody except Native Americans has the right to say anything about our immigration policy, because they are the only ones who have "always" been here. Whenever anyone suggests that we restrict immigration or reconsider our existing policy, ten voices jump in to recite Emma Lazarus's poem "The New Colossus," which imagines the Statue of Liberty saying, "Give me your tired, your poor, / Your huddled masses yearning to breathe free, / The wretched refuse of your teeming shore. . . . "

I can't tell you how many people have quoted this poem to me and then acted like they've won an argument. The Statue of Liberty wasn't erected as a flashing VACANCY sign to the most miserable people in the world. It was a gift from France to celebrate our nation's victory in the Civil War and to demonstrate our commitment to the cause of freedom. *Liberty Enlightening the World* has more in common with John Quincy Adams's statement that America is "the well-wisher to the freedom and independence of all. She is the champion and vindicator only of her own" than with an open invitation to the globe to bum-rush Ellis Island.

Now, it is true that most Americans are descended from people who came here from somewhere else. My great-grandparents came here from Ireland, at great expense and risk to themselves. They loved their new country and instilled a sense of patriotism in their own children. I am pro-immigration. America is made better and richer through immigration. We are among the most generous and expansive in the world in terms of letting people come here. No other nation is so open to admitting and naturalizing millions of people so consistently, and most Americans agree that immigration is a net positive.

But I'm talking about legal immigration. Legal immigrants wait years to come here, fill out extensive paperwork, and undergo background checks. When they get here they have to wait around seven years, pass tests, pay taxes, stay on the right side of the law, learn English (in theory), and vow allegiance to their new country. Legal, orderly immigration adheres to and promotes the rule of law.

Illegal immigration undermines the rule of law. It is a form of line-jumping and mocks the system of laws that legal immigrants abide by. It tells our whole society that it's okay to ignore the most fundamental rules about the American character. It creates a shadow society and a caste system that insults our traditional beliefs about equality. Illegal immigration promotes an America that is more of a check-cashing and payday-lending storefront than a nation.

Our immigration system is not "broken," as Democrats like to say. What they mean by that is that it is necessary for us to grant citizenship to the tens of millions of illegal immigrants currently here so they can be registered to vote. What is broken is our system of enforcement, both at the border and in the interior. We have all the laws we need on the books to deal with the problem. What we lack is the will.

Advocates for illegal immigrants and the continued deterioration of our borders say that it's heartless and selfish for people who descend from immigrants to "pull up the ladder" and deny other people the opportunity to pursue the American Dream. But that argument doesn't make sense, for a host of reasons.

First of all, America was not founded by "immigrants" but by settlers and colonists. There was no existing economy or culture here that welcomed the Pilgrims. They built it as they went along. People who came to America in the nineteenth and early twentieth centuries can properly be called immigrants, but the country they came to was radically different from the way it is now. The nation was growing rapidly, with an industrial economy that needed millions of low-skilled workers. There were no government programs to help the poor.

Furthermore, the nature of public policy is that it changes as circumstances and times change. In 1880, children could work in coal mines and textile mills, but society has decided that that's not a good idea anymore. In 1900, you could bottle a mixture of strychnine and opium and sell it openly as a cure for rheumatism, but then we passed laws regulating drugs. Just because our immigration system used to function in a certain way, that doesn't mean we mustn't change it, even when the population is many times larger than it used to be.

America today does not need low-skilled labor. Our farms and factories—such as still exist—are highly mechanized. More and more jobs require technical knowledge and training. In fact, with the influx of no-skilled immigrants from Latin America and other places, we have begun inventing jobs to give them something to do. In New York City, food delivery guys on "e-bikes" zip down the sidewalk, easily going 25 miles per hour. A few years ago, you might get food delivered from local places occasionally, but now it has become standard to order from distant places all the time.

We have a massive social safety net that transfers trillions of dollars from high earners to needy people, as well as providing a comfortable retirement for the aged, who paid into the system for decades. It's one thing to let people come and try to make a go of it when their failure will only cost them. But it's not clear why Americans should be expected to cover a foreigner's risk.

When someone comes to America legally, he almost always has a "sponsor," someone who promises to be financially responsible for the immigrant should things go badly. When Michael Bloomberg became mayor of New York City, his administration decided to send bills to the sponsors of immigrants who had needed to accept welfare or other forms of government assistance. Most of the sponsors made good on their obligation. But when Bill de Blasio came to City Hall, he decided that the requirement was inhumane. He stopped sending out notices, and then reimbursed all the sponsors for any money they had paid to cover the costs of their sponsored parties' welfare.

That sums up the attitude of the Left regarding immigration, both legal and illegal. The job of Americans is to make sure that immigrants are happy and comfortable. If they get in trouble, we will pick up the tab. Anything else would be a betrayal of "who we are," as progressives love to say.

## WHO GETS TO COME HERE?

It wasn't always this way. Starting in the mid-1920s, the United States began to limit immigration. Over the previous forty years, the country had admitted millions of immigrants, increasing the percentage of the population that was foreign-born to 14 percent. The United States Congress voted in 1924 to take a breather on letting in more people, in order to let the country absorb millions of new Americans, and encourage the adoption of national values.

The impulse to set limits on immigration was driven by multiple factors. On one hand, there was a nativist strain. After the bloodshed of World War I, when 117,000 Americans were killed in about eighteen months, and another 200,000 wounded, many felt the United States should turn inward. The country had also experienced a wave of radical political violence by anarchist terrorists, many of whom were immigrants. In 1920, for instance, a horse-drawn wagon blew up outside the New York Stock Exchange on Wall Street, killing forty people and injuring hundreds more. An Italian anarchist called Mario Buda was implicated in the act.

But organized labor also supported the restriction of new immigrants. Samuel Gompers, an English Jew who had immigrated to New York with his family as a teenager, became a major labor leader in America and founded the American Federation of Labor, which eventually evolved into the AFL-CIO. He supported the restrictive Immigration Act of 1924 because he knew that capital used the importation of unskilled labor to drive down wages.

It's commonly said that the 1924 Immigration Act was racist. This claim was the core of the argument made forty years later to undo the act. But it's a fact that the 1924 act, while restricting immigration from southern and eastern Europe, imposed no limits on immigration from Mexico or anywhere else in the Americas.

Ten percent of the population of Mexico came to the United States between 1910 and 1929.

It used to be commonly understood that immigration hurts American workers. Nowadays this perspective is mocked as something that rednecks and losers say—*"Immigrants take our jerbs!"*—but it was always a basic tenet of the labor Left, as opposed to today's woke Left. It is a little-known fact that Cesar Chavez, the founder of the United Farm Workers, saw illegal immigrants as strikebreakers, opposed laws that would make it easier for migrant workers to cross the Mexican–U.S. border, and even sent his members to confront illegal aliens at the border! Chavez would have applauded Trump's plans to build a wall.

The period of restrictive immigration between 1924 and 1965, incidentally, coincided with a period of economic expansion for the middle class that was unique in human history. The twenty-year period after World War II saw the working class, which could finally set terms on an equal basis with capital, prosper enormously. This was a period when a man with a high school education and a solid factory job could earn enough to raise a family, own a house and a car, and live a comfortable life.

In 2015, when Bernie Sanders was fighting Hillary Clinton for the Democratic nomination, he was asked if he favors open borders. "Open borders!" he exclaimed. "No, that's a Koch brothers proposal," he insisted, referring to the libertarian billionaire industrialists whom the Left sees as the root of all evil. The "Koch brothers," one of whom died in 2019, were conservatives who contributed a lot of money toward their favorite causes, including lower taxes and more free enterprise. But they were not dogmatic Republicans. They also supported drug decriminalization, were pro-choice and pro–LGBT rights, and supported criminal justice reform. Many Democrats were outraged at the idea that leftist Bernie would oppose open borders, which sounds so idealistic, like something out of a John Lennon ballad. "Imagine there's no countries, it isn't hard to do. . . ."

This godless vision of the world is sickening to most normal people.

If they knew anything about the history of their own movement, they would have understood. Sanders is an old-fashioned labor socialist. His ideology is wrong, because socialism is always a failure, but at least he doesn't promote all the woke dogmas about how whites are essentially evil. The new woke Left hears "open borders" and all they can think of is a gloriously diverse rainbow of new Americans coming to take over the country that rightly belongs to them anyway. Hence the chant that we heard across America after Trump took office: "No borders, no nations! F--- your deportations!"

## THE BLACK LESBIAN DEMOCRAT CONGRESSWOMAN FROM TEXAS WHO WANTED TO CLOSE THE BORDER

Old-fashioned leftists often have more in common with the MAGA Right than many Democrats would care to admit. In 1994, President Bill Clinton appointed former Democrat congresswoman Barbara Jordan to be the chair of the U.S. Commission on Immigration Reform. Jordan was a black woman from Houston who became the first African American elected to the Texas state senate since Reconstruction. A staunch liberal and feminist, she supported the Equal Rights Amendment, and is believed to have been the first lesbian to serve in Congress.

The conclusions of the Commission on Immigration Reform, known commonly now as the "Jordan Commission," sound like something you might hear at a Trump rally. It found that immigration most profoundly affects native-born high school dropouts, who then accounted for 10 percent of the workforce, reducing their wages by around 5 percent, but that there are other costs that cause stress, particularly on local communities.

The report suggested that the United States cut legal immigration by at least a third; eliminate "chain migration," which lets immigrants steadily bring in dozens of relatives in the name of "family unification"; focus on admitting high-skilled applicants and eliminating the visa lottery; and, most importantly, structure our immigration policy to favor the country, not the immigrants who wish to come here. "We disagree with those who would label efforts to control immigration as being inherently anti-immigrant," explained the report. "Rather, it is both a right and a responsibility of a democratic society to manage immigration so that it serves the national interest."

It is no stretch to say that the words *national interest* no longer have any place in the debate about immigration, at least among the Democrat Left, for whom the idea of putting America first is the essence of racism.

Jordan's report demanded that the government increase enforcement on the border and within the country. It did not shy away from insisting that deportation is an important tool. "Credibility in immigration policy," it explained, "can be summed up in one sentence: those who should get in, get in; those who should be kept out, are kept out; and those who should not be here will be required to leave."[1]

It is a great loss that Barbara Jordan died in 1996, shortly before the report came out. We lost a great advocate and champion of the cause of law and order as it pertains to the national interest and American prosperity. One only can wonder what she would have said about Trump and his platform, which owed much to Jordan's hard work.

All the perverse actions of the woke Left make sense if you take into account their hatred for America *as it is*. Figures like Barack

Obama or Hillary Clinton will cloak their distaste for America and existing Americans with reference to an idealized version of the nation. Obama spoke of the need for "fundamental transformation" of the United States. That's just a polite way of saying "revolution." If you love something, you don't want to turn it into something "fundamentally" different.

Remember the cheesy Billy Joel song with the lyric "I love you just the way you are"? Imagine rewriting it to say, "I love you just the way I want you to be." Loses something, doesn't it?

Part of changing America involves changing the people who live here. A consequence of the 1965 Hart-Celler Immigration Act has been the rapid decline of the country's white population. Now, this in itself is neither good nor bad. But when the politics of the Left have been based in an "antiracist" ideology of white guilt and the implicit moral superiority of nonwhite groups of people, we see that the question of racial diversity is not neutral. The Left has promoted diversity as a tool of electoral division, and continually celebrates the declining white population as evidence of the death of the old America, and the need to replace it.

This political narrative of "white replacement" has been called a conspiracy theory that white supremacists employ to justify racism and violence. But the same people who call it a false conspiracy theory celebrate it. The *New York Times* ran an opinion item called "We Can Replace Them." Democrat Dick Durbin, chair of the Senate Judiciary Committee, exulted that the "demographics of America are not on the side of the Republican Party. The new voters in this country are moving away from them, away from Donald Trump, away from their party creed that they preach."

If the Left talks about demographic change, they are celebrating diversity. If the Right points out the same facts, they are stoking hate and division. That's why discussions about immigration are so heavily weighted. Any hint or suggestion that our national interest is not served by letting anyone and everyone come here is immediately cast as racist and xenophobic. We understand why the Left is so intent on suppressing debate and getting as many immigrants in the door as possible.

## THE WALL

When Donald Trump put illegal immigration front and center in his presidential campaign, he lit a fire under the Left. Trump's election gave his political opponents a cynical opportunity to pretend that he was planning a massive racial cleansing of the United States.

Even before Trump's descent down the Trump Tower escalator when he made his now-famous announcement speech, the Left was fighting a low-key war against immigration enforcement across America. During the Obama years, leftist activists around the country worked overtime to stop local law enforcement agencies from cooperating entirely with federal immigration authorities, in what they characterized as a natural extension of their "sanctuary" policies.

The idea of sanctuary cities for illegal aliens was embraced, somewhat unexpectedly, by then-mayor Rudy Giuliani in the 1990s. The idea then was to assure illegals that the cops weren't out to bust them for immigration violations. There was some sense to this policy. If illegal aliens were afraid to talk to cops at all, then they would never come forward as witnesses or even victims of crime. This would encourage criminals to target their neighborhoods. Also, it didn't make sense to dissuade illegal immigrants who got sick from going to the hospital, or from sending their kids to school.

But the idea of maintaining the NYPD as a neutral force regarding federal immigration violations wasn't enough for the radicals. The police and the Department of Corrections still cooperated with the feds when it came to detaining illegal aliens who had committed serious crimes. U.S. Immigration and Customs Enforcement (ICE) maintained a presence on Rikers Island and were informed when illegal aliens entered the city's criminal justice system. The city would inform ICE, which would issue a "detainer," or a request to hold the criminal alien to be transported to an ICE facility where their deportation could be arranged.

Nonprofit organizations from the extreme Left, funded by George Soros, agitated for the city to expel ICE from Rikers Island, refuse to honor detainer requests, and cut all ties with federal immigration authorities, unless the illegal alien in question was on the terrorist watch list or had recently been convicted of murder or rape—and then, only if a judge had signed a warrant. Otherwise, criminal illegal aliens would be released back into the community to continue their depredations. "Sanctuary" would no longer indicate a kind of "Don't ask, don't tell" reaction to immigration status, but an explicit umbrella of protection against federal law on the part of radical cities and even states. New York elected officials and activists applauded the proposal as a demonstration of local values.

New York City passed this legislation in 2011. Around the same time, the state of Arizona passed a law with the opposite intention. Federal law already requires noncitizen immigrants to carry their identification papers with them at all times; Arizona SB 1070 made it a crime to be present in Arizona without carrying the documents, and required law enforcement officers to determine the immigration status of suspects during legal stops. The law barred cities or counties from refusing to enforce federal law. SB 1070 was the most vigorous state-level immigration enforcement law in the country. It was seen as an effective way to discourage illegal immigration across the border into Arizona, and it would encourage illegal aliens to go home, or to another state. The law was applauded by local activists, who saw it as a way to defend American sovereignty at a time when Obama's Washington was failing to do so.

The emerging woke minority was animated by the Arizona law, too. They sprang into action on multiple fronts. Major protest marches were held in Phoenix, Los Angeles, and other cities. Protestors staged demonstrations and committed "civil disobedience" outside the White House. Various liberal congressmen made the usual comparisons to Nazi Germany. Many prominent rock stars swore they would boycott Arizona. Several large cities vowed to stop doing business with companies headquartered in Arizona.

Obama's Department of Justice sued the state of Arizona. The case wound its way to the Supreme Court, which ruled against Arizona on key points, finding that the state law was an illegal preemption of federal statute. Justices Antonin Scalia, Clarence Thomas, and Samuel Alito dissented, with Scalia arguing that "as a sovereign, Arizona has the inherent power to exclude persons from its territory, subject only to those limitations expressed in the Constitution or constitutionally imposed by Congress. That power to exclude has long been recognized as inherent in sovereignty."

Right after he took office, Trump imposed a moratorium on travel from a handful of countries associated with state-sponsored terrorism. This was labeled the "Muslim Ban," and outrageous lies were told about it. In New York, hundreds of nonprofit staffers, elected officials, lawyers, and protestors raced to the airport to offer aid to some desultory travelers, who were held up and celebrated as victims and survivors of a racist attack.

It was at this moment that the Left's coordinated reaction to Trump's victory became clear, as nonprofit groups brought suit against the administration in front of friendly federal judges in distant jurisdictions. Derrick Watson, a district court judge in Hawaii, became the go-to guy for radical opponents of immigration enforcement measures. Liberal judges routinely issued national injunctions blocking presidential executive orders, a practice that has questionable constitutional validity. Why should a district court judge, of which there are almost seven hundred, be allowed to veto the president?

Nationwide judicial injunctions were issued against the travel ban, against revisions to the travel ban, against the restriction of funding to sanctuary cities, against revisions to the census regarding citizenship status, against using funds to build a border wall, and against implementing a rule regarding asylum status, among dozens of other such injunctions. These injunctions were technically temporary and subject to appeal, but the process of appealing injunctions to the higher courts can take years, which is the point. The Left used the courts as a way to gum up Trump's efforts to implement his agenda.

It's funny that Trump was accused of being an authoritarian and a fascist. If he was an authoritarian, he must have been the least effective dictator in history. Every time a district court judge issued an injunction against executive branch policy, Trump accepted the delay and went along with the ruling, even though low-level judicial injunctions are arguably unconstitutional. Trump's respect for the rule of law was extraordinary, given that it was being weaponized to impede his authority.

## IMPORTING VIOLENCE

Mara Salvatrucha, known commonly as MS-13, is a Salvadorean gang known for its fantastic acts of brutal violence, especially as retribution or warning to other gangs. MS-13 is known for wiping out entire families, including women and children, in acts of revenge. The public, extravagant nature of their violence plays out in the United States, too. Los Angeles, Long Island, and the Washington, D.C., area are hotbeds of MS-13 activity, and have seen gruesome murders by gang members. In the first three months of 2016, MS-13 was identified with seventeen murders on Long

Island. The group is involved in child prostitution, money laundering, drugs, contract killing, and any other nefarious activity you care to imagine, on multiple continents.

Federal enforcement efforts against MS-13 go back to the George W. Bush administration. In 2004 the FBI created the MS-13 National Gang Task Force, which by 2011 had effected three thousand arrests of MS-13 gang members. Among cops and other criminal justice professionals, it's never been a secret that MS-13 is a major public menace. But when President Trump took aim at the gang as an example of why the country needs better immigration enforcement, the media and top Democrats suddenly said that the threat of MS-13 was overblown, and that the whole thing was an excuse to smear all illegal immigrants as savages.

House Speaker Nancy Pelosi took issue with Trump's characterization of MS-13 members as "animals." She explained her belief that

> we're all God's children. There's a spark of divinity in every person on Earth and that we all have to recognize that as we respect the dignity and worth of every person. . . . And so when the president of the United States says about undocumented immigrants, "these aren't people, these are animals," you have to wonder, does he not believe in the spark of divinity? The dignity and worth of every person? "These are not people, these are animals," the president of the United States. . . . Calling people "animals" is not a good thing.

Not everyone knows that Nancy Pelosi's brother was charged with a bunch of his buddies in a gang rape of a twelve-year-old girl in 1953 in Baltimore. Pelosi's dad, who was the mayor of Baltimore at the time, attended the trial every single day. All of her brother's friends went to prison. Her brother was the only one who was acquitted. This is the kind of background Nancy Pelosi comes from—where lies and influence are all that matter.

Joy-Ann Reid, the MSNBC host, criticized Trump for calling MS-13 members "animals," saying he had concocted MS-13 as a bogeyman to scare his base. "He makes it sound like the biggest issue in the United States, or the biggest threat is MS-13, a gang nobody that doesn't watch Fox News has ever heard of," Reid insisted. "For this president to conflate the Dreamers with gang members, he was demonizing our immigrants here, and I was offended."

The *Los Angeles Times* fretted that Trump had "seized on" MS-13 gang killings "to justify [an] illegal immigration crackdown." The paper quoted Patrick Young, program director of the Central American Refugee Center on Long Island, as saying that "Trump is using [MS-13] to terrorize the immigrant community." In 2019, the *Washington Post* sniffed that calling MS-13 a "savage gang" is going over the top, because their killings were actually going down. Two years later, Biden's Department of Justice added Yulan Archaga Carias, the head of MS-13's Honduran operations, to the FBI's Ten Most Wanted List.

In the federal law enforcement cosmos, ICE does not have the glamour, funding, or reputation of other agencies. It isn't part of the vaunted "intelligence community." It doesn't take down many international criminals or bust open major drug- or sex-trafficking rings. But ICE does the dirty work that many in our ever-softening society would prefer to ignore. ICE agents arrest serial deportees who return again and again to our society to prey upon the very old or the very young. ICE does the nasty job of keeping our country safe by removing people who are not supposed to be here.

## "ABOLISH ICE"

A key tenet of the Left, as spelled out in Saul Alinsky's classic 1971 manifesto *Rules for Radicals*, is to personalize your political opposition in order to mobilize around a specific figure. "Pick the target, freeze it, personalize it, and polarize it," Alinsky wrote. In combatting Trumpian fascism, the Left picked ICE as a primary target, and set about demonizing the agency, disrupting its activities, and raising the personal cost of operating as part of the organization.

Starting in 2017, "Abolish ICE" suddenly emerged as a new slogan. News database searches reveal that this phrase had never been used prior to the summer of 2017; after that, its use exploded. This is typical and expected. Leftist messaging works in a highly coordinated fashion, and we often see slogans or protest themes catch fire across media and other outlets all at once. "It's Time to Abolish ICE," announced Sean McElwee in the *Nation* magazine in March 2018.

The article quotes a variety of nonprofit "policy directors" and "civil rights" attorneys all to the same point: that "ICE as it presently exists is an agency devoted almost solely to cruelly and wantonly breaking up families," in the words of Dan Canon, who was also engaged in lawsuits against Donald Trump for "inciting violence at his rallies."

"Groups like Indivisible Project and the Center for Popular Democracy have also called for defunding ICE. Brand New Congress, a progressive PAC, has the proposal in its immigration platform," we are told. The Center for Popular Democracy and Indivisible are both Soros-funded projects of the Open Society. Brand New Congress is the political action committee (PAC) that sponsored Alexandria Ocasio-Cortez's run for Congress.

"Public outrage over the Trump administration's 'zero tolerance' border policy, which separated thousands of families, has intensified the skepticism over immigration enforcement. 'Abolish ICE' is becoming a catchall rallying cry against draconian immigration policies," liberal website Vox explained in June 2018. The theme of "family separation" became central to the "Trump Resistance," though any American who breaks the law with his child in tow is equally subject to "family separation," because we don't send children to adult prisons.

No matter. ICE became popularly equated with the Nazi Gestapo, and its abolition became a major cause for Democrats and everyone to their left. "I think there's no question that we've got to critically reexamine ICE and its role and the way that it is being administered and the work it is doing," Kamala Harris told MSNBC, repeating the key talking point. "And we need to probably think about starting from scratch because there's a lot that is wrong with the way it's conducting itself, and we have to deal with it."

Opposing ICE quickly evolved into attacking ICE agents. Sam Lavigne, an "artist" and professor or fellow at New York University, Columbia, the New School, and most recently the University of Texas, "doxxed" 1,600 ICE agents and published a database of their identifying information. This project received praise from both Antifa and supportive media sources.

An image of a crying child standing next to a Border Patrol agent was described by national publications and major television news programs as documentation of forced family separation, even though it eventually emerged—awkwardly—that the little girl in the picture was not in fact separated from her mother; she was just crying. "Kids in cages" became a rallying cry across the country, and drew public officials to the border to decry the Obama-era policy. Congresswoman Alexandria Ocasio-Cortez was photographed weeping and clutching a fence that was ostensibly penning in desperate migrants, even though it really just led to an empty road. Spineless New York City mayor Bill de Blasio similarly stood next to a fence in South Texas looking sad.

These clowns run a circus that's short on peanuts, elephants, a ringmaster, and a net. But that doesn't stop them from screaming in your face and making you cry.

De Blasio pulled a similar stunt when ICE indicated that it planned to arrest known illegal aliens who had already been given orders of deportation that they had ignored. The mayor called a major press conference at the New York City Department of Education where he announced an action plan to blockade ICE agents from entering school buildings, where they would supposedly seize children to deport them. When asked how many times ICE agents had ever approached a New York City school to arrest a child, he conceded that it had never happened. His press office later edited the video of the press conference to delete that question and answer.

Manufactured outrage against ICE was mounting in the summer of 2018. In Portland, Oregon, and across the country, Antifa and its useful idiots embarked on a series of blockades of ICE facilities. In Portland, protestors set up a camp outside the building and refused to permit any vehicles to enter or leave the facility. Similar protests took place in Manhattan, Los Angeles, Detroit, Philadelphia, and Atlanta. In Portland, local police refused to help clear the illegal encampment, in another show of support for local anarchists over the forces of order. Eventually, federal officers came to the aid of the besieged ICE officials, and the encampment was broken up.

At exactly the same time, three Democrats in the House introduced legislation to shut down ICE entirely. "President Trump has so misused ICE that the agency can no longer accomplish its goals effectively," Congressman Mark Pocan of Wisconsin said. "The best path forward is this legislation, which would end ICE and transfer its critical functions to other executive agencies."

Note how similar this language is to the type of rhetoric associated with the "Defund the Police" movement that blew up two years later. The advocates say that the problem is with the institution, which is so rotten that it must be dismantled entirely. They promise that the function will still be carried out, more effectively, by reallocating resources. But in both cases, what the radicals really want is to hollow out criminal justice in pursuit of their real end, which is to destroy America. Why would you shut down the agency that performs immigration and customs enforcement unless you want to end immigration and customs enforcement? And why would you end immigration enforcement unless you want to see America disappear?

## HEROES ON HORSEBACK

Probably the most grotesque and cynical attack on the integrity of the men and women who protect the homeland—the actual territory of the United States—came in the autumn of 2021, when tens of thousands of Haitians illegally crossed the U.S. border at Del Rio, Texas. Totally overwhelming the Border Patrol capacity, the illegal immigrants set up camp and waited to be processed. In August, Haiti had suffered a double blow of an earthquake and a hurricane, and the island's economy and infrastructure were devastated, with thousands dead.

The humanitarian crisis in Haiti and the sudden arrival of tens of thousands of Haitian migrants at the U.S. border with Mexico were connected, but indirectly so. These migrants weren't victims of the earthquake. Rather, they had been living in Brazil, Argentina, and other countries in Latin America for many years. When disaster struck their homeland, they made a beeline north, assuming that the United States government would admit them and give them "Temporary Protected Status" (TPS).

Whenever something terrible happens somewhere in the world, the U.S. government is typically pressured by advocates to allow illegal immigrants from that region to remain in the United States on a "temporary" basis, which often stretches out for years or even decades. Haitian expats shrewdly calculated that they could exploit the misery of their home country to pose as refugees at the U.S. border. That's why they didn't run for the interior after they crossed the border at Del Rio: they were waiting to register themselves as refugees, which would grant them legal status and the ability to work and obtain benefits.

While they waited, the "refugees" went back and forth across the Rio Grande into Mexico, where the shopping was cheaper. The image of thousands of Haitians crossing the river and setting up camp shocked Americans watching on television, and brought home the reality of the border crisis. Biden ran in 2020 on the promise that he would halt deportations and revise Trump's policy of prohibiting illegal immigration. After he was elected, the number of people apprehended at the border tripled—the number who got through is unknown, but is estimated in the hundreds of thousands per month.

In an effort to maintain some order, mounted agents of the Border Patrol were assigned to perform crowd control and monitor the area. When patrolling the banks of a meandering river and its brushy floodplain, it makes sense to use horses. Some pictures were taken of the horsed agents in the proximity of Haitian border cross-ers, and were quickly spread on social media and news programs as evidence that the agents were being "cruel, inhumane," and "in violation of international law."

One of the horsemen was photographed apprehending an ille-gal alien while holding the reins of his horse; activists and politi-cians who had clearly never been on a horse claimed that the agent was "whipping" the migrant. A furor erupted. "Shocking images of horse-mounted officers corralling Haitian migrants along the US–Mexico border," reported the BBC, "are evoking dark compari-sons to US slavery and the country's historical mistreatment of black people."

Similarly, the *New Yorker* magazine explained that "images of mounted U.S. Border Patrol agents driving Haitian migrants away from U.S. territory evoke comparisons to slave patrols of the early eighteenth century." Progressive "Squad" member Congresswoman Rashida Tlaib of Michigan complained that "cracking a f—ing whip on Haitians fleeing hardship shows you that this system simply can't be reformed," and her colleague Alexandria Ocasio-Cortez, who knows a thing or two about feigning outrage at the border, commented, "Our immigration system is designed for cruelty towards and dehumanization of immigrants." Vice President Kamala Harris proclaimed, "What I saw depicted, about those individuals on horseback treating human beings the way they were, is horrible. . . . [H]uman beings should never be treated that way and I'm deeply troubled about it."

President Biden joined the scrum, calling the action "outrageous" and thundering, "I promise, those people will pay. There is an investigation underway right now and there will be consequences." Usually, when there's an investigation, we wait until it's done before demanding consequences. But in this case, the decision to use the border agents as political pawns to distract from Biden's own failed border policies—which have seen dozens of known terrorists get stopped at the border and then released into the United States—trumped the need for due process.

None of these critics bothered to ask photojournalist Paul Ratje, who took the pictures of the agents on horseback trying to deal with thousands of illegal migrants, what he had actually documented. "Some of the Haitian men started running, trying to go around the horses," Ratje explained. "I've never seen them whip anyone. He was swinging it . . . but it can be misconstrued when you're looking at the picture."

It's hard to believe that the president of the United States would stoop so low as to throw agents of the Border Patrol—who perform fantastically difficult and dangerous work—under the bus in order to serve a cheap, flimsy political narrative. But when demonizing law enforcement is a key element of your party's platform, there are evidently no limits.

# CHAPTER EIGHT

## Politicizing the Military and Federal Law Enforcement

ON JANUARY 6, 2021, CONGRESS MET to certify the electoral vote count as submitted by the states. That day at noon, Donald Trump sponsored a "Save America" rally to encourage his supporters to keep up their legal challenges to Biden's election, which he called "a disgrace." President Trump went step-by-step through the many ways in which the 2020 election had major anomalies that deserved inspection. He called on Congress to reject votes from the states where the election had been conducted in what he called—and many legal scholars agreed to be—an unconstitutional and illegal manner, including major, last-minute changes to balloting procedures, like allowing mail-in voting on demand, or loosening signature requirements, or letting politically aligned "community groups" go around "harvesting" ballots and submitting them by the trunkload.

Was Trump calling for an overthrow of the U.S. government? No way. The democratic process is a process, which means there are a series of steps that have to be carefully attended to. Demanding that the law be followed is not a "coup."

Listen to what Trump had to say. Does this sound like violent, revolutionary talk?

> Now it is up to Congress to confront this egregious assault on our democracy. And after this, we're going to walk down—and I'll be there with you—we're going to walk down. We're going to walk down any one you want, but I think right here. We're going to walk down to the Capitol, and we're going to cheer on our brave senators, and congressmen and women. And we're probably not going to be cheering so much for some of them because you'll never take back our country with weakness. You have to show strength, and you have to be strong.
>
> We have come to demand that Congress do the right thing and only count the electors who have been lawfully slated, lawfully slated. I know that everyone here will soon be marching over to the Capitol building to peacefully and patriotically make your voices heard.

Trump called for his supporters to protest and to exercise their constitutional right to peaceably assemble and call for a redress of grievances. To say otherwise is to say that the rule of law doesn't matter, and that the American people have no right to question their masters in Washington, D.C.

While Trump was still speaking, a crowd broke off and marched to the Capitol. We have all been subjected to endless replays of the protest there, elements of which became a riot. In sum, about two thousand protestors entered the Capitol building and "occupied" it for a few hours. While inside, a few participants stole trophies, including a podium and Nancy Pelosi's laptop. By and large, however, their occupation of the Capitol was calm. You can see video where they are looking around respectfully, like tourists. Once inside, they basically didn't do anything.

The experience of the crowds on the outside of the Capitol was mixed. Some protestors got into fights with officers of the Capitol Police who were blocking their entrance into the building, but other protestors were clearly admitted to the Capitol without any confrontation. There are many videos showing Capitol Police moving barricades aside and waving the crowds through and into the building. There is even footage of a protestor inside the Capitol trying to open a door to let others in. The door seems to be electronically locked. The protestor appears to wave at a security camera, at which point the door is unlocked, and he opens it to let people in. Why did someone in a remote security office unlock the door at a protestor's behest, if the protest was a violent invasion?

There are a lot of questions about January 6 that have been unanswered—and even *unasked*. But one thing is clear: it was not an insurrection. It was not a violent attempt at a coup, even if some protestors fought with the cops. What kind of a coup attempt ends after a few hours when its participants decide to go home?

In the context of the entire previous six months of rioting, destruction, murder, and arson, the January 6 demonstration was nothing exceptional. Billions of dollars of damage were inflicted on cities across the country, and tens of thousands of cops were injured during the 2020 George Floyd riots, according to the FBI's own statistics. Mobs burned down police stations in Minneapolis and Portland, and tried to destroy Portland's federal courthouse. A pair of lawyers in New York City were caught throwing firebombs at occupied police vehicles. Hundreds, if not thousands, of radical anarchists crossed state lines in order to commit acts of terror. If the Department of Justice wanted to, it could implicate a huge number of people in a massive conspiracy aimed at death and destruction.

While a few of these radicals were arrested and prosecuted for their individual acts of violence, the federal government did not in fact launch a massive investigation into "antifascist" networks. They didn't release hundreds of hours of footage, and ask the public to help identify protestors and arsonists. They didn't imprison hundreds of people, many in solitary confinement, nor did Congress hold special hearings to implicate government officials in giving aid and comfort to rioters. But the FBI and the Justice Department, which have effectively become political tools of the Democratic National Committee, did all of that, and more, in its all-out confrontation with the January 6 riot.

The Democrats have put all of their energy and hopes into promoting the myth that January 6 was a unique moment in American history. An attempted coup by white supremacists and other fascist elements was averted, they say, even though there is no indication that the protestors had any real plan to overthrow anything, nor that the "insurrection" ended for any reason other than its participants got bored and left.

America was subjected to congressional hearings in the summer of 2021 that went on for days, with members of the Capitol Police weeping about what they suffered on January 6. Whenever I find myself in a discussion about January 6 with one of the rare individuals who believe the narrative that it really was an insurrection and a coup attempt, I am always informed that "police were attacked!" Now, it is true that some officers were injured on that day, and that's obviously nothing to celebrate.

But who promised the Capitol Police that they would never have to deal with a riot? Crowd control and policing protests are a basic duty of law enforcement. They are trained in it and it's an expected part of the job. I am 100 percent in favor of law and order and believe that people who attack police officers should be prosecuted. I think that the people who mobbed the Capitol were foolish. But the endless parade of crying about Capitol Police officers is ridiculous. So *now* the Left is a fan of the police? None of the people—Pelosi and company included—who are so horrified by the actions of the mob on January 6 expressed anything but satisfaction when police were attacked throughout the George Floyd summer extravaganza. As Pelosi said then, "People will do what they do."

The Department of Justice under Biden has dedicated itself to tracking down and arresting anyone who entered the Capitol on January 6—and even people who weren't anywhere near Washington, D.C. Hundreds of people who did nothing more than walk into the Capitol—in some cases after having been waved in by Capitol Police—have languished in jail, some in solitary confinement. Many have been denied bail. Attorney General Merrick Garland indicates that he plans this investigation to go on for years.

In June 2022, the House Select Committee to Investigate the January 6th Attack on the United States Capitol presented its initial findings in a Hollywood-produced "hearing" during prime time. The House Republicans were barred from selecting their representation on the committee, an unprecedented action by Speaker Pelosi, who named only vociferous anti-Trump Republicans to speak for the party they reject. All of the major broadcast and cable channels cleared the decks for this two-hour propaganda program. For a week ahead of time we were told that we would finally see video footage that had been held back because of its sensitive, inflammatory nature. Finally we would see the horror of January 6, up close and unedited.

What we wound up seeing was more of the same stuff we had seen before: protestors marching on the Capitol and scuffling with police. A couple of windows were broken. A mock gallows was set up outside the building; this was supposed to serve to hang Vice President Mike Pence, except in reality it was only about three feet tall. The committee laid out its case: The January 6 riot was an earnest attempt to overthrow the government of the United States and illegally install Donald Trump as president. Trump himself was behind this plan, along with a group of conspiring lawyers including Rudy Giuliani. Trump called for the January 6 rally, and encouraged his followers to invade the Capitol by any means necessary and force the Congress to elect him president.

Probably the best summary of the whole dynamic was made by a political outsider. Jack Del Rio is the defensive coordinator for the Washington Commanders (formerly known as the Redskins). Asked about some comments he'd made about the riot at the Capitol on his personal Twitter account, Del Rio explained:

> I can look at images on the TV [of the Floyd riots]—people's livelihoods are being destroyed. Businesses are being burned down. No problem. And then we have a dustup at the Capitol, nothing burned down, and we're going to make that a major deal. I just think it's kind of two standards, and if we apply the same standard and we're going to be reasonable with each other, let's have a discussion.

For stripping the whole narrative stark naked with such blunt common sense, the sports media—which in many ways is worse than the regular news and political commentary when it comes to pushing the woke social justice agenda—went crazy. Every ESPN show had to air a lengthy "explainer" demonstrating why Del Rio was "lying," or "spreading misinformation" about how the 2020 George Floyd "protests" were actually much worse than the insurrection. It looked like Del Rio might lose his job, but instead he was forced to apologize and was fined $100,000 by his team.

And for all the talk about how "deadly" January 6 was, let's not forget that only one person was killed that day, and she was an unarmed veteran shot by a cop. To my eye, Ashli Babbitt posed no threat to the safety of Capitol Police lieutenant Michael Byrd when he fired his pistol into her neck, killing her. Byrd was cleared of wrongdoing by the Justice Department and the Capitol Police, though his actions may have gotten him fired and prosecuted in other circumstances or jurisdictions. He was lionized as a hero by the media and the Democrats, who decided that, in this one instance, it is glorious when unarmed protestors are killed by the police.

The exploitation of federal law enforcement by Democrat presidents has become normal, but Biden, or whoever is running things, has taken it to a depraved low. Under Obama, you may recall, they sicced the IRS on hundreds of "Tea Party"–style patriotic groups, targeting them for special investigation. Then Obama and the Hillary Clinton campaign coordinated to spy on Trump's campaign and concocted the whole Russia treason fantasy. But under Biden the politicization of the FBI and other federal entities has become like something you might expect to find in a failed state. The American government is now turning into the type of regime that routinely imprisons whoever was in power yesterday, like Bolivia or Pakistan.

The Democrats concocted a theory based around the January 6 riot that Trump and his associates planned to prevent Biden's election, remain in office, and thus overthrow the government. Their evidence for this is that Trump and his team got together to discuss how to challenge corrupted election returns in states where there was a question about whether the election was legitimate. John Eastman, Trump's lawyer, has been accused of orchestrating a coup through a demonic scheme to get then–vice president Mike Pence to refuse to count the electoral votes. The Department of Justice seized Eastman's phone and his indictment is widely expected. But all Eastman did was write a memo explaining the constitutional process and the role of the vice president in certifying each state's votes, and sketching out various possibilities of what to do if the election is corrupted. According to Eastman, Vice President Pence was not required to rubber-stamp the counting of the electoral votes, but had the responsibility and duty of considering whether the votes were valid.

On January 6, 2017, when then–vice president Joe Biden was certifying the electoral votes for Donald Trump's election, Democrats interrupted the proceedings eleven times to object to the certification of electors. Congressman Jamie Raskin, who served as a key manager of Trump's impeachments, objected to ten of Florida's electoral votes on the grounds that they "violated Florida's prohibition against dual office holders." Representative Barbara Lee objected to Michigan's votes, saying, "People are horrified by the overwhelming evidence of Russian interference in our election."

On January 6, 2005, California senator Barbara Boxer and Ohio congresswoman Stephanie Tubbs Jones objected to the certification of Ohio's electoral votes in George W. Bush's successful re-election bid over the hapless John Kerry. Boxer listed an array of supposed electoral irregularities and said she was objecting in order "to cast the light of truth on a flawed system which must be fixed now." Nobody called Boxer or Jones traitors or said that they were destroying democracy by claiming that the election was flawed or fixed.

On January 6, 2001, while Congress was certifying George W. Bush's electoral victory over Al Gore, a dozen congressmen tried to block Florida's votes on the grounds that black voters there had

been disenfranchised. Their objection was overruled, and their protest is seen as a valiant effort to rescue what all faithful Democrats
agree was a stolen election.

Were all these Democrats trying to overthrow the government by bringing up weird technicalities and absurd conspiracy
theories?

Anyway, if John Eastman's ideas were so seditious and trou-
bling, why is it that a bipartisan group of senators has proposed
legislation to make the role of the vice president in counting the
electoral votes purely ceremonial? The Electoral Count Reform
and Presidential Transition Improvement Act will "establish clear
guidelines for our system of certifying and counting electoral votes
for President and Vice President." But this admits that the current
system is actually complicated and really does have "loopholes" that
they want to close! So Eastman must have had a point.

Whether Trump's lawyer was right or wrong about his legal
opinion, he's entitled to give it. Imagine if we start arresting lawyers
for what they tell their clients.

Steve Bannon, Trump's advisor, was found in "contempt of Congress" for refusing to testify before the House January 6 committee.
Being found in contempt of Congress normally doesn't amount to
anything, but in this case, Bannon was arrested by the FBI and tried
in federal court, where he was found guilty. Bannon was sentenced to
four months in federal prison. Peter Navarro, another Trump advisor,
similarly refused to testify before the committee. He was indicted,
and the FBI arrested him at the airport, shackled him, strip-searched
him, and refused to let him speak to his lawyer. These are extraordinary actions—normally in such cases men in their seventies with no
criminal record are simply asked to come to court.

After months and months of beating the drum about January 6,
the Dems started to get tired of pushing their narrative so relentlessly, with so little payoff. Basically, outside of Beltway circles and

Democrat hysteroids, no one believes the story. I live in deep-blue Manhattan, and talk to a lot of people. I have never encountered one single individual whose salary isn't dependent on promoting the insurrection fable who has said anything about it. And as we move farther away from the incident—whaddya know? There hasn't been any follow-up to the supposed attack on "Our Democracy." Usually a violent insurrectionary conspiracy doesn't just dissolve itself after an afternoon. So where is the ongoing violence?

So the Dems and their FBI attack dogs picked a new strategy. In August 2022, the Department of Justice staged a raid on Mar-a-Lago, Trump's residence in Palm Beach, Florida. They broke open his safe and combed through wife Melania's clothes closet, seizing a number of boxes of documents. Everyone assumed they were looking for records relating to January 6 and the effort to overturn the election, but no, they were on to something new. This time they claimed that Trump had retained "Top Secret" classified information related to "nuclear weapons."

This raid on a former president's house was totally unprecedented in American history. It's the craziest thing I have ever seen. Naturally the poodle press picked up the hint and started fantasizing that Trump had stolen America's nuclear secrets in order to sell them to our enemies.

It's obvious to me what's going on here. They needed a new narrative to add to the giant pile of manure they have already concocted about Trump. So they get a compliant judge to sign a warrant, raid his house, seize a bunch of files, and that's enough to leave everyone thinking that there's much more to the story than we know.

Acting as a kind of Praetorian Guard for Democrat-elected officials, protecting the reputation of Joe Biden's children has become an important mission of the FBI. In April 2019, Hunter Biden left his laptop with a computer service repair shop and never returned to pick it up. Among other material, the laptop contained emails demonstrating that Joe Biden, contrary to his public statements, had been involved in his son's business dealings with foreign entities in Ukraine and China. The owner of the repair shop evidently informed the FBI about the laptop, and the agency seized it in December 2019.

News about the laptop broke right before the election in 2020, and was immediately and massively suppressed by social media companies, apparently in conjunction with the Biden campaign. They insinuated strongly that the laptop was fake. The FBI indicated that they were investigating whether the laptop and the reporting about it were part of a Russian campaign to influence the election. Later, after Biden won, everyone acknowledged that the laptop was real. It went from being a giant hoax perpetrated by Russian disinformation agents to being true, but of no interest to the media and FBI, even though the laptop demonstrated that Biden was intimately aware of his son's shady dealings.

Ashley Biden, Joe Biden's daughter, evidently left some bags at a former roommate's house in Florida. Someone went through her stuff and found her diary, which contained personal information about her family's weird sexual dynamics. The diary found its way to the hands of conservative muckraker James O'Keefe, whose organization Project Veritas is famous for running stings on Planned Parenthood and other liberal organizations. The Trump campaign expressed no interest in exploiting the diary for campaign purposes, and advised Project Veritas to give the diary to the FBI, which it did. But then, in 2022, the FBI raided the offices of Project Veritas and the homes of its employees, claiming they were investigating the theft of the diary. But the diary had gone astray from Ashley Biden's hands well before the election, when her father was a private citizen. Why was the FBI so vigorously pursuing the question of this missing diary, even to the point of harassing the journalistic organization that had given them the diary in the first place?

This goes well beyond any abuse of federal law enforcement authority we've ever seen in America. The FBI isn't the personal protection force for elected officials, even the president. But they are now behaving like a mob boss's thugs, going around to harass anyone suspected of crossing the "big guy."

Legal harassment of Trump supporters takes place at multiple levels of prosecution. In New York State, Attorney General Letitia "Tish" James has taken aim at the Trump Organization, insisting that it had misled lenders—many years before Trump ran for office—about the value of collateral it was putting up for loans. This was clearly a politically motivated prosecution, because nobody had noticed it or cared about it before Trump became president. The companies that Trump allegedly defrauded never complained. The whole thing was cooked up to get revenge on Trump for winning.

Rooting through your enemy's past and looking for ways to put him in jail is the sort of thing that goes on in dictatorships. "Show me the man and I will find the crime" was the maxim of Joseph Stalin's top prosecutor. When Tish James ran for attorney general, she made exactly the same promise.

New York pressed ahead with its prosecution of Allen Weisselberg, the former chief financial officer of the Trump Organization. Weisselberg faced lengthy jail time because he failed to report certain perks he got as a corporate officer, including use of a company car and some other fringe benefits, as income. The total alleged "tax fraud" amounts to maybe a few hundred thousand dollars. This is the sort of thing that is almost never prosecuted at the state level, and it is usually considered a civil matter, demanding at most that the culprit pay a fine.

But the prosecution of Weisselberg certainly looks like legal blackmail to force him to "spill the beans" on his former boss. This is evil. It is one thing to prosecute the underlings of a known criminal in order to get him to flip. But in this case, they don't even have anything on the boss: they want the underling to come up with charges against the guy they want to put in jail.

In the wake of the January 6 riots, the federal government announced that countering white supremacists would be the primary focus of domestic law enforcement. Shortly after the Biden administration came into power, the Pentagon declared that "extremist" white supremacy is a major threat inside the military. Attorney General Garland and Secretary of Homeland Security Alejandro Mayorkas similarly insisted that extremists "who advocate for the superiority of the white race" are the "greatest domestic threat" facing the United States.

As I have said before, "white supremacy" is idiotic, as are all forms of racism. You have to be stupid as a can of peas to imagine that your skin color makes you better than someone else. So we should all count ourselves as blessed that, for all intents and purposes, there aren't any white supremacists of any account running around the country. At least, none that anyone can identify. For all the talk about white supremacy at the Capitol on January 6, I have yet to see any evidence that any of the people arrested there were expressing racist views, or that they were motivated by white supremacy. Nor do I see any evidence that white supremacists exist as a viable political force in America. People talk about the Ku Klux Klan like it is still an important movement. Well, if that's true, who's its leader? Where is their headquarters?

Two weeks after Biden's inauguration, Secretary of Defense Lloyd Austin ordered a "stand down" across the entire Defense Department to "discuss the problem of extremism in the ranks." While the "stand down" proposed to tackle all forms of extremism, in reality it served as the start of a political purge to remove

Trump supporters from positions of authority. Liberal rag *Vanity Fair* announced that "the new administration has promised not just to return things to where they were the day before Trump took office; it has vowed real progress on multiple fronts."

Secretary Austin established the "Countering Extremism Working Group," headed by Bishop Garrison, his top Diversity, Equity, and Inclusion officer. Garrison is a Democrat partisan who has stated publicly that Trump voters are necessarily racist. "Support for him, a racist, is support for ALL his beliefs," he tweeted. The scope of Garrison's job included the design of critical race theory lessons for all members of the military, and training supervisors and commanders on "'gray areas' such as reading, following, and liking extremist material and content in social media forums and platforms."

Purging the military of wrong-thinkers was just the start. Leftists have been clamoring to purge police departments across America of conservatives and patriots. The Brennan Center for Justice, a major left-wing public policy institute connected with New York University, and which has been heavily funded by organizations linked to radical billionaire George Soros, complains that bias training in police departments is not enough because it "leaves unaddressed an especially harmful form of bias, which remains entrenched within law enforcement: explicit racism."[1] The Brennan Center demands that the federal government begin investigating every use-of-force complaint nationwide "for indications that racial or ethnic bias motivated the violence," and to scrutinize social media postings by local officials for hints of unsavory opinions.

The Biden presidency is failing. The only hope the Democrats have of retaining power is to bring Trump—and who knows how many others—up on charges of sedition and have him sent to prison. To this end they have subverted the entire federal administration of justice and turned it into a political club they wield against their opposition. Of all the ways in which the Left has perverted the rule of law in America today, its obscene use of the legal powers of the federal government is the most corrosive and deadly.

# CONCLUSION

YOU MAY HAVE COME AWAY from this book with the sense that I am angry. Well, I am. Frankly, I am furious! The Left has gone to town dividing our country and enflaming racial discontent in order to leverage power for itself. They no longer concede that Americans share common ground regarding basic values. As Hillary Clinton famously put it, a substantial number of us are "deplorable," past hope of redemption.

The main issue that the Democrats have exploited is race. Now, some people might argue with me that the reason race is such a big issue is precisely that race really is a big issue! But twenty-five years ago, Americans of all colors believed that race was less a big deal than they do today. Yes, it's true—polls show that Americans in 1998 were more optimistic about the treatment of black people in society than they are today—and that's after we elected and reelected a black man as president, and elected a black woman as vice president.

In 1998, 44 percent of black people felt that they were treated less well than white people at work; today, that number has grown to 63 percent. About 55 percent of black people thought they were treated less well than white people by the police in 1998; today, it's 80 percent who feel that way. Remarkably, in 2008, 47 percent of black people were "very or somewhat satisfied" with their treatment in society. But by 2021, that number had fallen to 15 percent![1]

What happened in 2008? Hmm . . . oh yeah, that was the year Obama was elected. He ran as a uniter, and governed as a divider. He told black Americans that they had been dealt a bad hand, and that there really wasn't anything they could do to improve their situation, because white people were "structurally" invested in keeping them down. The guy is a first-class cynic, and couldn't care less about what happens to this country.

So what can we do? Where do we go from here?

First of all, I would recommend that you don't let the Left intimidate you about race. None of what they say about it is real. They want to back you into a corner and force you to apologize for invisible grievances, because once you've admitted your guilt, they've got you where they want you. That's why leftist journalists kept hammering on Trump to "denounce" white nationalism: because doing it once means you have to do it again, forever. Naturally, if you have harmed someone, you should cure the injury, but don't apologize just because someone demands it.

Along with that, don't be intimidated by uniforms. This may sound paradoxical, because this whole book is about respect for law and order, but as an ex–military officer I feel confident in telling you that people who wear uniforms in order to bully other people into submission—whether politically or by force—are cowards and rascals. Soldiers and police officers are not our leaders or our legislators. They are servants. The job they do is underappreciated and difficult, and they deserve our respect and cooperation. But when

people in uniform put themselves forward as political spokesmen—
as with the January 6 cops—that's the beginning of actual fascism.

Also, and this probably sounds kind of corny, but it's a good idea
to write letters to politicians and other people in charge if you have
complaints. Phone calls don't mean anything. Emails are deleted on
receipt. Internet comments are radio static. But letters, especially if
they are handwritten, get noticed.

Finally, though, it's important for us to organize, even if it's
against our nature. The Left is composed largely of losers who don't
have anything better to do than get together and complain. Conservatives have jobs, families, and churches to attend to. We prefer
to spend our free time doing something fun or useful. Liberals want
to "make the world a better place," while conservatives believe in
"minding your business."

But just as the squeaky wheel gets the grease, the people who
bang pots and pans and whine and screech the loudest appear to
get their way . . . at least until they have ruined society enough for
the sane people to wake up and do something about it.

It's like if an angry kid is standing there throwing pebbles in
his yard. You ignore him until he starts dinging your car. Then you
make him stop.

Well, we are past the point where the crazies and losers are toss-
ing pebbles at our car. They have broken the windshield, deflated
the tires, and are trying to rip out the distributor cap.

We've got to act fast. Voting is fine, but we can't assume that
voting will save us. We need to gather as like-minded citizens who
care enough about the future of our country to oppose the rabid
Left, which is set on shredding everything we cherish about our
beautiful country. The storm clouds are gathering, and the hour
grows late.

# ACKNOWLEDGMENTS

**THE IMPETUS FOR WRITING THIS BOOK** is to honor my father, Raymond Kelly, the longest-serving and most highly regarded police commissioner in New York history. He started with the New York City Police Department (NYPD) when he was twenty years old. Over the next fifty years, he did it all, from chasing bike thieves in Central Park to global counterterrorism. Along the way, he garnered a very unusual résumé for a police executive: heading a multinational police force in Haiti, earning two law degrees and a master's from Harvard, serving as Treasury undersecretary in the Clinton administration, fulfilling a year of combat in Vietnam as a Marine Corps officer, and achieving the rank of Marine colonel in the reserves. All while being a devoted husband and father.

I am very grateful that he married Veronica Kelly, my mother. So many blessings she bestowed on me, with her passion for reading and self-expression, her commitment to my education, helping me at the kitchen table with math, reading, and vocabulary, and introducing me to a world of possibility. I hope this book makes her proud.

My brother, Jim, has saved my life twice (see my next book). I thank him for being the best verbal sparring partner I've had the pleasure of knowing. We speak almost daily. Jim has been a tremendous mentor and an incredible friend.

I am hugely indebted to author and public intellectual Seth Barron. His shared passion for the issues that I hold dear has made this book possible. Our hours of discussions—marveling at the injustices and misconceptions created by the liberal media about law enforcement—helped create the narrative of this book.

I have enormous gratitude for my editor, Natasha Simons. Her passion for this project and her focus on the most critical issues affecting our nation are beyond belief. Her indefatigable approach to extracting the most from her writers has deeply impressed me, and I hope to have the honor of working with her again.

I know that my publisher Jennifer Long's belief in the project contributed greatly to the book being green-lighted and will be instrumental in its success. I am truly grateful for her business acumen and the opportunity that she has given me.

Simon & Schuster editorial assistant Mia Robertson must be acknowledged and applauded for her incredible attention to detail and tremendous effort in getting this book across the finish line. She shows an enormous capacity for grace and understanding while enduring the pressures of the publishing industry.

My agent, David Limbaugh, is a person whom I'm so humbled to know. Not only has he been an enthusiastic champion of mine, but his commitment to his faith and the most important issues of our time has been a great inspiration to me. I deeply cherish every conversation we have had, and I admire his unrelenting energy in promoting conservative values and their spokespeople.

Where would I be without my friends and mentors, Nelson DeMille, Bill O'Reilly, Mark Simone, and Doug Brunt? Our evenings together discussing everything from books to politics, entertainment, and history have brought me tremendous joy and have been great learning experiences. Your belief in me and my capacity to connect with an audience gave me the confidence to tackle such an enormous challenge as writing this book.

Another dear friend and colleague I want to thank is Maya Zumwalt. We worked together at Fox News, finding ourselves everywhere from war zones to the White House. Most recently, we have been collaborating on a podcast series that focuses on the issues we both care deeply about—law enforcement, faith, national security, and finding dignity in every person roaming this beautiful planet. Maya's belief in me has helped me through some of the toughest moments of my life. I couldn't have written this book or survived many of the other challenges I have encountered without her guidance and positivity.

I am deeply grateful to Chris Ruddy, the founder and CEO of Newsmax, and John Catsimatidis, the owner and chief executive officer of Red Apple Media. I thank them for the opportunity they have given me to speak to millions of Americans and people around the world about the issues I care most about. They have helped me find my voice and gather the momentum needed to write this book. They are two of the most important thought leaders in America.

Cardinal Dolan has been a deeply influential spiritual leader in my life. He has been there when my faith has been strong, as well as when it has wavered. I am grateful for his service and the kindness he has shown me and my family. At times, the process of writing this book has been challenging, and my connection with the cardinal and our Lord has given me the courage and tranquility to persevere.

I hope that I am speaking for everyone when I express my deep gratitude to every member of the law enforcement community and the U.S. military. Every day, they are endangering their lives to protect ours, and they should be held in the highest esteem by each and every one of us.

Finally, with tremendous love and tenderness, I thank my wife, Judith. She has always seen the very best in me and, in her own subtle (and sometimes not subtle) ways, helps me maximize my potential every single day. Judith is the mother of our two daughters, Annalise and Madeleine Kelly. They have played a pivotal role in inspiring me to write a book to defend—and, hopefully, fortify—the people who will be there to protect them, and their future children, when I no longer can.

# NOTES

## Introduction

1.      https://www.bbc.com/news/world-us-canada-61218611.

## Chapter One: Defunding the Police or Defending the Police

1.      https://twitter.com/JenniferNuzzo/status/1267885076697812993.

2.      https://www.northjersey.com/story/news/paterson-press/2020/0
3/22/paterson-nj-church-shut-down-outside-service-amid-coronavirus
-restrictions/2895656001/.

3.      https://www.wdrb.com/news/national/police-chief-association
-releases-number-of-officers-injured-nationwide-during-violent
-protests/article_db673920-34ab-11eb-9431-a3e24704f86a.html.

4.      https://abcnews.go.com/US/60000-offigone to cers-assaulted-202
-31-sustaining-injuries-fbi/story?id=80661264.

5.      https://www.statesman.com/story/news/2022/02/17/austin-settle-2
-hurt-police-during-black-lives-matter-protests-justin-howell-anthony
-evans-floyd/6820949001/.

6. https://www.ojp.gov/ncjrs/virtual-library/abstracts/national -advisory-commission-civil-disorders-report.

7. https://www.forbes.com/sites/andrewsolender/2021/03/25/makes -jim-crow-look-like-jim-eagle-biden-slams-despicable-gop-voting -restrictions/?sh=5deef51c2fa9.

8. https://www.electproject/org/election-data/voter-turnout-demographics.

9. https://www.whitehouse.gov/briefing-room/speeches-remarks/2022 /01/11/remarks-by-president-biden-on-protecting-the-right-to-vote/.

10. https://www.cbsnews.com/news/joe-biden-criticized-for-highlight ing-ties-to-segregationist-senator/.

11. https://acleddata.com/2020/09/03/demonstrations-political -violence-in-america-new-data-for-summer-2020/.

12. https://twitter.com/cbsnews/status/1267877443911778306?lang=en.

13. https://twitter.com/kamalaharris/status/1267555018128965643.

14. https://www.congress.gov/116/meeting/house/110938/documents /HHRG-116-JU00-20200728-SD037.pdf.

15. https://www.nytimes.com/2020/06/11/us/politics/trump-milley -military-protests-lafayette-square.html.

16. https://defundthepolice.org/alternatives-to-police-services/.

17. https://www.ojp.gov/ncjrs/virtual-library/abstracts/reparative -justice-towards-victim-oriented-system.

## Chapter Two: The Collapse of New York City

1. https://www.bjs.gov/index.cfm/dataonline/content/index.cfm ?ty=pbdetail&iid=7226.

2. https://www.pennlive.com/opinion/2015/05/poor_blacks_looking _for_someon.html.

3. https://www.city-journal.org/html/black-family-40-years-lies -12872.html.

4. https://www.brookings.edu/research/an-analysis-of-out-of-wed lock-births-in-the-united-states/.

5. Todd Kendall and Robert Tamura, "Unmarried Fertility, Crime and Social Stigma," *Journal of Law & Economics* 50 no. 1 (2010): 269–308, https://doi.org/10.1086/596116.

6.      https://www.manhattan-institute.org/philadelphia-violence-root
        -causes-crime-policing.

7.      https://www.theatlantic.com/magazine/archive/1982/03/broken
        -windows/304465/.

8.      https://www.theguardian.com/world/2015/feb/02/nypd-stop-and
        -frisk-keeshan-harley-young-black-men-targeted.

9.      https://en.wikipedia.org/wiki/Crime_in_New_York_City
        #Murders_by_year.

10.     https://nida.nih.gov/publications/research-reports/marijuana
        /there-link-between-marijuana-use-psychiatric-disorders.

11.     https://www.themarshallproject.org/2019/01/07/the-case-against
        -cannabis.

12.     https://americanmind.org/salvo/false-hope-for-new-york/.

13.     https://pix11.com/news/local-news/manhattan/jogger-mugged-at
        -gunpoint-by-group-in-manhattans-east-village/.

## Chapter Three: The New Religion of Antiracism

1.      https://www.heritage.org/poverty-and-inequality/report/the-war
        -poverty-after-50-years.

2.      https://www.researchgate.net/publication/332733778_Equity_
        inclusion_and_antiblackness_in_mathematics_education.

3.      https://equitablemath.org/.

4.      https://www.splcenter.org/news/2021/02/03/learning-justice-teaching
        -tolerance-changes-its-name-reflect-evolving-work-struggle
        -radical.

## Chapter Four: Obama's Divided America

1.      https://www.politico.com/story/2008/06/text-of-obamas
        -fatherhood-speech-011094.

## Chapter Five: Abolish Society: The Vision of BLM

1.      https://blacklivesmatter.com/about/.

2.      https://www.statista.com/statistics/262962/countries-with-the
        -most-prisoners-per-100-000-inhabitants/.

3.  https://en.wikipedia.org/wiki/List_of_countries_by_intentional
    _homicide_rate.

4.  https://www.statista.com/topics/7088/crime-in-sweden/.

5.  https://ucr.fbi.gov/crime-in-the-u.s/2018/crime-in-the-u.s.-201
    8/topic-pages/clearances.

6.  https://www.ojjdp.gov/ojstatbb/crime/ucr.asp?table_in=2&
    selYrs=2019&rdoGroups=1&rdoData=c.

7.  https://www.iwf.org/2022/04/01/rafael-mangual-on-the-crime-crisis
    -in-america/.

8.  https://www.city-journal.org/html/charlies-angles-14791.html.

9.  https://www.usatoday.com/story/news/politics/2021/03/07/usa-today
    -ipsos-poll-just-18-support-defund-police-movement/4599232001/.

10. https://www.sentencingproject.org/publications/a-25-year-quagmire
    -the-war-on-drugs-and-its-impact-on-american-society/.

11. https://www.prisonpolicy.org/reports/pie2022.html.

12. https://www.cnbc.com/2022/05/13/biden-tells-states-to-increase
    -cops-mental-health-programs-to-fight-crime.html.

13. https://www.washingtonpost.com/graphics/investigations
    /police-shootings-database/.

14. https://www.policemag.com/596346/half-of-surveys-very-liberal
    -respondents-believe-1-000-or-more-unarmed-black-men.

## Chapter Seven: Nations Are Their Borders

1.  https://cis.org/Report/Remembering-Barbara-Jordan-and-Her
    -Immigration-Legacy.

## Chapter Eight: Politicizing the Military and Federal Law Enforcement

1.  https://www.brennancenter.org/our-work/research-reports/hidden
    -plain-sight-racism-white-supremacy-and-far-right-militancy-law.

## Conclusion

1.  https://news.gallup.com/poll/352544/larger-majority-says
    -racism-against-black-people-widespread.aspx.